26

26

*A true account of love, friendship,
faith, and a supernatural move of God.*

Sue Lyons

Published by Wesley Branch Publishing Company, Asheville, NC
Wesley Branch logo designed by Michelle Cress

Cover design by Jon Brooks

Printed by CreateSpace, An Amazon.com Company

ISBN-10:0-9970177-1-6
ISBN-13:978-0-9970177-1-7

To~

My three sons: Sam, Josh, and Micah. You portrayed great strength and faith throughout Dad's crisis. This book is a tribute to you because you would not waver in the face of adversity.

And to those who wonder if God really cares about your distress and heartbreak. I want this story to give you the hope to seek God and allow him to touch your deepest pain.

Part 1

I cried aloud to the LORD,

and he answered me

from his holy hill.

Psalm 3:4 (ESV)

Chapter 1

Saturday, 7:50 a.m.

"God, I need you! Please don't let him die."

I sat in my living room as three teams of paramedics crowded into our small den less than twenty feet away. Like a bombshell, my tidy and comfortable life exploded into disarray in a matter of minutes. My thoughts swarmed with fear, uncertainty, and other desperate emotions.

"God! Please! Help."

Just fifteen minutes earlier my morning had begun routinely enough.

Saturday, 7:35 a.m.

Early dawn trills of chickadees and goldfinches were a soft backdrop to my thoughts as I lay in bed, thinking of how abundant my life was.

One week ago our family enjoyed the North Carolina Outer Banks with friends. The weather had been warm and sunny. We had taken walks on the beach, enjoyed a dolphin cruise, crabbed, fished, and generally made the most of a beach vacation. Now we were back home in Asheville, North Carolina and I was mentally planning my morning. Jeff, my 57-year-old husband, and I made great improvements the day before on a rental unit we were preparing for future tenants. Our three teenaged boys would join us later in the morning after a sleepover with friends. The sunshine and Carolina-blue sky held great promise for a summer Saturday of teamwork.

These quiet musings were shattered by guttural sounds of distress coming from the other end of the house where Jeff had just ventured after a nagging cough had prematurely awoken him. Alarmed, I ran as quickly as I could and found my husband slumped back on the couch, his dark brown eyes open, yet vacant and unmoving. His cheeks and lips had a bluish cast and it appeared he had stopped breathing. I tried desperately to shake him out of his sluggishness, with no response.

With shaking hands I made the 9-1-1 call and a unit was dispatched to our small neighborhood. As I waited, the well-trained dispatcher kept me engaged and aware of any changes in Jeff's condition. Though his gulping breaths were only coming every 20 seconds, each one filled me with a nervous relief. I could hear a heartbeat through his chest and though I had been trained in CPR the last thing I was prepared to do was perform it on the man who lay before me.

Upon the dispatcher's instructions, I wrestled Jeff from the couch onto the floor, a hard surface that might ease his breathing struggles.

"Where are they? What's taking so long?" I frantically asked the man on the phone.

"They are on their way," he assured me with a calm, soothing voice.

Less than 10 minutes and what seemed a lifetime later, the rescue squad arrived and began the process of caring for their patient.

When I heard one paramedic confirm a heartbeat, I felt the tentative hope that my strong and active mate would be fine soon. However, as equipment was set up and baseline data secured, the atmosphere drastically changed. Urgency filled the young medic's voice as he announced, "I've lost his heartbeat! The patient is in cardiac arrest. I am beginning chest compressions."

My husband had just died.

Chapter 2

More paramedics arrived and rushed into the small den to try to save Jeff's life. I knew the best place for me was in an adjoining room. As I glanced one last time toward my husband of 18 years, all I saw were his two bare legs laying white and limp, the rest of his body shielded by the forms of rescue personnel. I knew what they were doing and I couldn't watch.

So here I was, pleading with God, urgently asking for his intervention.

Numbly I sat on our couch, vaguely aware of people coming and going. I gathered my thoughts.

"God," I prayed, "You have never let us down. In every crisis you have been faithful. Please, take care of us."

Despite my shock, I had a deep sense of assurance that God would meet all of our emotional and physical needs no matter what happened today. He would give us the strength we needed to face the future, no matter what that future entailed.

Yet, at the same time, my thoughts were sporadic. My mind was making leaps between praying in faith that God would revive Jeff's heart, and wondering where the life insurance information was stored. While listening for signs of success from the other room, I was mentally listing local funeral homes.

I wondered about our teenage sons, Sam, Josh, and Micah. If Jeff couldn't be revived, what would they miss in their lives without their dad? How could I ever fulfill the vital role he had? Had it been a mistake to let them stay with friends last night, knowing they could have said "I love you, Dad," one last time?

"Oh, Lord," I pled, "These boys *need* their father! Please help the paramedics pull him through."

My attempt to contact my dearest friend who lived close by was met by a recorded message, she and her family likely gone for the weekend. Though I was outwardly calm, I felt vulnerable and desirous of the presence of someone who knew us well and trusted God deeply. *Who do I call and how can I find their phone number?* My mind went blank. *How can such a basic task become so difficult?* Finally, a name and phone number came to me and I called one of our pastors. He and his wife lived 15 minutes away.

A cheery voice answered, pleased I had called on such a beautiful Saturday morning. The message I conveyed with my soft and shaking voice was not what Pastor Rick's wife, Amy, was expecting: "Jeff's heart has stopped beating. The paramedics are doing CPR, but I think he has gone on to be with Jesus. Please come be with me. I don't want to be alone." There was dead space for a matter of seconds as she processed the news. Though in a state of disbelief, Amy assured me that she and Rick would be on their way as quickly as possible.

As I hung up, I suddenly thought of a friend across the street who would give me the comfort I needed. Why couldn't I think of her a minute ago? After a shocked response to my phone call and situation, Phyllis came over to endure the wait with me. She wrapped her arms around me as we sat quietly on the couch. Her prayers gave me reassurance that God was in the midst of this situation and his power more than adequate to strengthen, guide, and give wisdom to everyone involved.

Every few minutes, the EMS Captain Brian, came and compassionately kept me apprised of the situation. I knew the likelihood for Jeff's survival diminished with each passing minute.

We waited. A chaplain sent from the fire department came and prayed for Jeff. I politely listened. He seemed to be an intruder to a very personal situation. After all, how could a perfect stranger know how to pray for my husband?

As I was thinking this, the house grew eerily still and quiet. My heart also stilled as I braced myself...

I began sobbing as I heard the following message: "It is 0-8-14 and the patient's heart has begun beating on its own."

Jeff had survived 26 minutes of CPR.

Chapter 3

Relief overwhelmed me. I hugged Phyllis and could barely get the words out that Jeff was alive. My body began trembling as I prayed, "Thank you, God! Thank you, God!" The seemingly impossible had been done. Rarely had the crew revived a patient after a cardiac arrest, never after 26 minutes. But that wasn't on their minds at this time; keeping him alive was.

The next several minutes were a blur of calculated and well-rehearsed actions. Jeff was transferred to a gurney and prepared for the journey to the hospital. Now that his heart was beating on its own, it was critical that he be transported to specialized care as quickly as possible.

Brian once again came to me and patiently explained the process. "The medics are putting ice packs around your husband in order to lower his body temperature. At the hospital it will be brought down to 91 degrees Fahrenheit for at least 24 hours."

He must have seen my questioning look.

"Let me explain," said the Captain. "A few people, especially children, have survived drownings of up to an hour submerged in icy waters. The body shuts down the brain's need for oxygen, delaying possible brain damage. The heart can rest by not beating as fast. Medical staff try to mimic the same by artificial cooling. Outcomes from this procedure have been promising in the case of cardiac arrest victims."

He stood. "As soon as we can, we'll get him into the ambulance." Brian disappeared into the den while I processed the fact that Jeff was alive and I needed to get ready to accompany him.

Shortly thereafter, the gurney rolled past me, guided by two medics. For the first time since the EMS crew had arrived at our house, I laid eyes on my husband. He was covered with a heavy blanket, an oxygen mask helping him breathe, in his arm an IV. He looked exceptionally pale and still. My relief of a few minutes prior was replaced by a wave of distress. Phyllis squeezed my arm.

As I watched him pass by, a voice broke through to my consciousness: "We *will* hear a good report on your husband," the fire department chaplain stated emphatically as he gained my attention. His eyes held conviction. Those were the last words I heard upon leaving our house.

Jeff was loaded into the waiting ambulance as I was helped into the passenger seat. Our residential road was clogged with rescue vehicles. Concerned neighbors, our friends, were milling on their front lawns, anxiously watching the proceedings and carrying on subdued conversations.

Just as we set off with siren wailing, I noticed Pastor Rick and Amy pulling to the curb. They came expecting to comfort a widow. As they stepped out of their car, confusion, then hope, filled their faces as they recognized that an ambulance with lights flashing, hurrying to the hospital, could only mean one thing: Jeff was still alive. They hurried back to their car to follow.

Our next stop was the Emergency Room.

Chapter 4

If I had been in a less serious state of mind, I might have enjoyed the sight of cars scattering as we sped toward the hospital. But as I saw curious faces peering at us as we whisked by, I wondered how many times I had watched an ambulance drive past and not given much thought to the circumstances. Who was in the back: a daughter, a father, a friend? Was a family afraid or devastated, their world turned upside-down in the matter of minutes? Had I even been mindful of the dedication of rescue personnel, at least two in the back of each ambulance, skillfully caring for patients? Now *I* was the one in the passenger seat. *I* was the one who had a precious loved one being ministered to by the paramedics in the back. *My* husband was the one clinging to life. I resolved to never again gaze at an ambulance en route to an emergency with indifference.

Upon arrival to the Emergency Room, the gurney was unloaded and wheeled to awaiting nurses. My husband and the medical staff administering his care disappeared behind cold metal doors which stated in bold letters: "Emergency Personnel Only." The doors clanged shut, a barrier that seemed to close me off from the most important person in my life. The ambulance driver guided me to the waiting area, a large, comfortable, yet quiet room. I was alone.

I wondered how long it would be until Rick and Amy arrived. After all, they would have been held up at each red light our ambulance had been able to rush through. Their presence would have given me comfort.

A security worker manned the door to the Emergency Room, waiting for the authority to allow visitors in to see the patients within. He assured me it would only take ten minutes or so for Jeff to be admitted. Not sure what to think, what to hope, or how to pray, I waited. Just 12 hours earlier the two of us had been sharing a pizza and watching a movie, enjoying a tired feeling of accomplishment. Now a cruel kind of emptiness took its place. As one so quick to plead to God when others need intervention, I was strangely quiet on my own husband's behalf.

At last, the doors were opened so I could finally join him. I walked past several occupied rooms, as I made my way to 7A. The curtain was pulled closed so I pushed it aside to enter the cubicle. When my eyes fell on the breathing tube, IVs and other assorted wires and monitors attached to him, the gravity of Jeff's condition was suddenly real. Involuntary shivering wracked his body as it cooled. His eyelids were barely cracked open, revealing staring, vacant eyes. The nurse assigned to Jeff's care was monitoring the various screens filled with information such as heart rate, oxygen level, and body temperature. As I entered, she gave me a sympathetic smile. I moved to his side and held Jeff's hand, cold and still in my own.

In a matter of minutes, Amy arrived and moved quietly to my side to offer support. Appreciative of her presence, I was nonetheless struggling with this scenario. I felt empty and helpless.

The nurse asked questions concerning the events surrounding Jeff's cardiac arrest: Was I there when it happened? *Yes.* Did he have any prior complaints of pain or discomfort in his chest? *No.* Does he have a family history of heart disease? *No.* How is his general health? *Good, aside from a nagging cough due to asthma.* Does he have any allergies? *Grass, mold, and aspirin.* And a myriad of others that she needed to know to best to care for him.

I answered each with a calmness and confidence that masked the undercurrent of my emotions. In truth, I felt overwhelmed. My future, which up until two hours ago was busy but predictable, was now filled with the unknown. When a radiology technician stepped in to take Jeff for X-rays, Amy and I retreated to the waiting room to try to make sense of what was happening.

Chapter 5

Emerging from the ER into the waiting area, I was taken aback by the group of people who had come to bring support. Of course, Pastor Rick and Amy had arrived shortly after the ambulance, but there more familiar faces; those whom had sacrificially forgone their weekend plans to be here. The small group was growing rapidly, many from our church, some neighbors, and all familiar friends. A staff member graciously allowed us our own waiting room.

Matter-of-factly, I gave them my version of the morning's events. I felt able to hold my distress in check until one of our closest friends, Dan, arrived. When I saw the concern and love in his eyes, the pent-up feelings of sorrow and uncertainty overwhelmed me. Just as my brother would do, he held me tight and allowed me to unleash my emotions. Just two days prior, Dan and his wife had hosted our family for a wonderful evening of fellowship and prayer. Now we were meeting under quite different circumstances; the contrast seemed unjust.

As my sobbing subsided, I sank to the chair, clasping my hands and looking at the faces of those gathered. No inspiring verses of promise filled my head or heart. No confident prayers bubbled up to the surface ready to call on the mercies of God. Unable to find the strength to exercise my own faith, I relied on my friends to stand for me. And they did.

The group began to pray. They asked for mercy. They asked for healing. They asked for God to give all of the doctors and nurses wisdom and skill to do their jobs. They asked for God to be glorified through Jeff's time in the hospital. They asked that God would touch the hearts of many, to convey his love to them. Ultimately, they asked that God's perfect plan would be accomplished even in the face of such struggle.

My mind was firm in the knowledge that God is powerful, loving, and involved in the lives of his children. When the Bible states "Nothing is impossible with God," I wholeheartedly agree. Yet in this case I was uncertain how God's purpose would unfold. My mind kept straying to fear. Thankfully, our friend, Tad, father of a Navy SEAL and always strong in the face of adversity, sensed this, and came and knelt before me.

He took my hands in his. "Look at me, Sue," he implored. "Look me in the eyes and listen."

I gave him my attention. I could tell easily that Jeff's situation had taken a toll on Tad, and his voice quavered when he spoke. But I saw the resoluteness in his eyes as he boldly stated, "The doctors may have a diagnosis for Jeff, but God *always* has the final say. Jeff is alive now, so apparently God is not through with him yet. Your job is to stand by him and stand by those three young men of yours."

My three sons. Until this time I'd been hesitant to let them know what was happening to their dad. All they were aware of was that he wasn't feeling well so the workday had been cancelled. It was time to let them know the truth. Three of the men volunteered to get them from our friend's home and bring them to the hospital. There couldn't have been three better choices: Tad, along with Patrick, our church's worship leader, and Caleb, a faith-filled young man. The boys loved and respected all three. It would take at least an hour to retrieve them and return. I prayed they would experience faith, not fear.

As I thought about Tad's statement, another man from our church arrived. With a tender smile and excitement in his eyes, Rod shared that his wife, Joy, had seen a vision of Jesus standing next to Jeff's hospital bed, protecting him. Joy said it was so real it was as if she could reach out and touch them both. She was convinced that Jesus would see Jeff through this crisis and he would live to tell about it.

By now Jeff would be back from getting his X–ray. Armed with this arsenal of prayers, words of faith, and a vision from God I was ready to stand by Jeff's side.

Chapter 6

This time when I walked into Jeff's cubicle I wasn't as dismayed by his situation. My friends and their prayers had reminded me of God's power and ability to make this awful situation into something valuable. God has a purpose in all we go through, the good and the bad. Besides, I made a promise to my husband nearly nineteen years earlier that I would stand with him in sickness and in health.

"Why don't you talk to him?" suggested the nurse assigned to Jeff. "Some patients that wake up from a coma say they heard what loved ones were saying to them." She spoke with kindness as she looked me in the eyes. "Speak to him as if he was awake."

I moved forward and held his hand. Could my words make their way into the deep recesses of Jeff's thoughts, even in a coma? If so, I wanted my words to be loving, encouraging, and filled with truth. Looking into his still face, I explained he was in the hospital, well taken care of. As I told him about our friends and church family gathering in the waiting room, I found my voice. I continued on: "You are stable and the doctors will get you into your own room soon. The boys are coming to see you. They should be here soon. I love you, Honey, and will be here for you." I spoke these details into his ear with tenderness as if he could hear me, all because a nurse gave me hope and an important purpose.

Then, for the first time that morning, I really prayed for Jeff: for his healing and restoration and for God to be honored by this event. I prayed for each doctor and nurse that would be assigned to him, not only that they would think clearly and use their God-given skills with precision, but that God would hand-pick each one perfectly for Jeff's situation. I thanked God that he was already moving in this crisis and that nothing was out of his care.

It wasn't long before the ER doctor came in to update me on Jeff's condition: although he had experienced a cardiac arrest his pulse and blood pressure were good, a good sign. He'd apparently had a heart attack, but they wouldn't be sure until blood tests came back. Though the X-ray detected pneumonia, that didn't account for his cardiac arrest. He'd been put on the "Arctic Sun", a device that would slowly bring his body temperature down to 91 degrees for 24 hours. In the meantime he was in an induced coma and would be started on paralyzing medication that would stop his body from shivering. He was stable and ready for an ICU room. It might be a long time before they would know the side effects of his extended cardiac arrest.

The doctor also conceded, "The paramedics that performed CPR did an outstanding job. They are the reason your husband is still alive."

I wholeheartedly agreed, though I thought to myself that God had a plan as well. At this point I just didn't know how it would turn out.

Chapter 7

My phone vibrated and I was informed that the boys were in the waiting room. I squeezed Jeff's hand, kissed him on the forehead, and whispered that the boys were here. We would see him in his room as soon as he was settled. Drawing in a deep breath I told myself to be strong and encouraging. My sons needed a parent to give them hope and faith.

As I walked into the waiting room, all three were surrounded by our friends. Sam, 16 and most tender-hearted, had tears in his eyes as he hugged me. I could tell he was doing his best to hold his emotions in check. Josh, 15 and always stoic, gave me a hug as well. He held on longer than usual, a real sign of support to me. Micah, 13, and most outgoing of the family, was handling his uncertainty by telling one-liners and humorous stories to the friends gathered.

People filed out of the room so I could privately relate to the boys some of the details of their dad's situation. There was good news with the bad news; Dad was stable. I reminded them of the high quality of care Mission Memorial Hospital was known for. The doctors and nurses are exceptional with access to state-of-the-art equipment. Most importantly, I reminded them of what we stood by as a family: God loves us, has good plans for us, and will never forsake us. Nothing is impossible with God.

"God will carry us through, no matter what," I emphasized.

"I know." The straight-forward statement came from Josh. When we turned our attention to him he explained:

"The *iPlay* bag was between the seats in the van and I could read the words on it. All I could see were the words "I AM" facing me. I knew that was God telling me that he was taking care of Dad. Once I saw that, I knew everything would be all right."

I marveled at the depth of his faith. I was trying to be strong for him and he ended up being the one who spoke a confident faith into me! Josh was referring to a reusable grocery bag Jeff had received from the company where he worked that makes baby clothes and accessories. The bag is decorated with about 20 light-hearted sayings about children. One says: "I play therefore I AM." It had been used to transport items the boys took to their friend's home and tossed into the van when leaving for the hospital. I was newly astonished at how God truly was involved in this crisis and ready to strengthen and comfort us even through small details.

Relieved that the boys seemed to be handling this difficulty, we all geared up for whatever was ahead.

Chapter 8

We didn't have long to wait. A man in blue scrubs came and led us through a labyrinth of hallways as we made our way to the "Heart Tower" and the Cardiac ICU. We were shown yet another private waiting room that appeared to be designed for overnight stays. Before going to see Jeff, I did my best to prepare the boys for what they would see: a breathing tube, monitors, IVs, and an unresponsive father.

"You don't have to go," I reminded them. "Seeing Dad this way will be upsetting. I'll leave it up to you."

Remarkably, all three wanted to see their dad, despite the discomfort and fear of what they would witness. After following the protocol of hand-washing, we walked past the ICU desk and found Jeff's room, shrouded by a thick, sliding curtain. Within, we could see the movements of two nurses tending to Jeff's needs. Upon our arrival they opened the curtain to allow our entry.

Jeff lay still on the bed. Now he had thick blankets covering him. The boys stood, pierced by what they saw. The soft "swoosh" sounds of the breathing tube, and the "beep-beep" of various monitors filled the room.

I moved up to Jeff's side and gently picked up his hand. "Hi, Honey, it's me. You're in the cardiac ICU now and getting great care. The boys are here to see you." I explained to them what the ER nurse had told me about patients in a coma remembering the words of loved ones upon waking. "Would you like to speak to him?" I asked.

Watching their faces, I could see the struggle, yet the resolve to support their father. Sam was the first to move forward, put his hand on Jeff's arm and pray silently for him. Josh was the next to move, resting his hand on the blankets. Micah hung back and observed, struggling with the whole scenario.

With all of his seeming jocularity, Micah was taking this medical emergency the hardest. His bond with Jeff was special. He was the one who most enjoyed the "rough and tumble" father/son relationship. So many times laughter would fill our home as Micah tried to outdo his dad with wrestling moves. As Micah continued to get bigger and stronger with age, the matches would become longer and more intense. Each ultimately ended with both gasping for breath, red faced, but glad for the good-natured competition. How could his strong, fun-loving dad be helpless and on life-support?

I couldn't answer the questions I suspected roiled in his mind. I was thankful he had friends to spend time with when he wasn't at the hospital, who would help get his mind off of the situation until he was ready to face it.

We returned to the waiting room. By now our entourage had made it to the Cardiac ICU. Despite Jeff's situation being so dire, the atmosphere was uplifting. The boys and I settled into the comforting embrace of our supporters.

As it neared noon, the boys decided to go home and get a few things they needed to spend the night with friends. I asked Josh to load some Christian worship music onto our laptop. If it was true that people in a coma could hear the voices of loved ones, how much more powerful it would be for Jeff to hear the beautiful music and words extolling God's love and power.

I felt torn to see them go but knew these sons of mine needed some time to settle into the reality of this new situation facing them.

Chapter 9

After the boys left, I returned to the waiting room. The room was outfitted to seat six comfortably, so our large group spilled out into the hallway. Due to visitation restrictions, only two were permitted in Jeff's ICU room at one time. So, two by two we went to support and pray for him. The initial reaction upon seeing Jeff for the first time was similar for each person: stopping, looking at him in disbelief, gathering composure then walking up to him to pray out loud or silently. By now a neurological technician had added about a dozen electrodes attached to Jeff's head with long wires leading to yet another monitor. It was a disconcerting sight. Every time someone came I would walk to Jeff's side, hold his hand and let him know who was visiting and praying for him. My natural, conversational tone seemed to put people more at ease. Everyone shared a Bible verse, an encouraging phrase, or a prayer for God's healing and grace.

The Bible includes a verse that says the word of God will not return void. I believed that every verse and prayer said over Jeff would have a consequence. God was hearing every single one and responding in deep care and love. Would Jeff be healed and whole quickly, or would it be weeks or even months before he was strong again? Or would he only be healed in Heaven, when he would be completely renewed? I couldn't know. In the meantime, while waiting, I would trust that God was lovingly responding to the pleas on Jeff's behalf.

Early in the afternoon, I remembered a dear friend that worked at the hospital as a respiratory therapist. Alvin could be counted on for support and prayer, so I texted him to see if he was working today. A few minutes later I received the disappointing news from his wife, Joni, that the family was out of town and Alvin wouldn't be back to work until the middle of the week. I quickly filled her in on Jeff's plight. A minute later I heard the "ping" of my phone. Joni sent me the encouraging news that Alvin had heard of cases when people had recovered with no ill effects after more than 30 minutes of CPR.

That news bolstered my determination to pray for Jeff and trust God. It was one thing to pray knowing God can do anything, relying completely on faith and nothing else. It is an emotional boost to pray knowing that recovery is not only possible, but has happened before to others.

Shortly after 1:00 p.m., the boys returned to visit and drop off the items they had gathered from home. Josh handed me a large bag. Aside from the laptop and a pillow, I found both my Bible and Jeff's, along with his reading glasses. I almost laughed.

"Josh, you sure have a lot of faith!" I declared. Once again I was astounded. I was not about to tell him what was in my mind, that it could be a long, long time before his dad would be able to read. Even if God helped Jeff recover, I had seen the doctor's projected release date written on a large white board: 30 days, and tried hard to not think of why they projected such a long-term recovery.

Before my sons left to spend the rest of the day with good friends, we set up the laptop which Josh had installed to play many of Jeff's favorite worship songs. All of the songs Josh had chosen spoke of God's love, power, and yes… healing. As the music softly played, and in the relative quiet of the room, I took time to reevaluate my own perspective. Perhaps I needed to apply Tad's admonition: *"The doctors may have a diagnosis but God has the final say…"* Yes, in black and white the board said Jeff's projected release date was 30 days. But hadn't God healed the blind, the lame, and the deaf in an instant?

I held Jeff's hand, listened to the music, and worshipped also.

Chapter 10

The difficult chore of making personal phone calls to family was inevitable. All of our extended family lived several hundred miles away. Amid the whirlwind of emotional decisions I had been making over the past few hours, thoughts of contacting them had been pushed aside. Naturally, I desired to spare them from emotional pain and worry. Wondering about the best timing to break the bad news, I even considered waiting; perhaps tomorrow would bring more encouraging results. Recognizing my frayed emotions were over-running common sense and family bonds, I reached for my phone. After all, Jeff's life was precarious. I needed to let family know what had been happening. Concluding that now was the right time, I began the task by calling Jeff's family members.

His parents lived in northwest Indiana, and as I shared with them the shocking news of their son's condition, I tried my best to soften the blow. They listened in disbelief as I explained details, carefully putting forth the most positive aspects of the day so far. To their credit they took the news calmly. Despite their being in a state of shock, I ascertained they were doing their best to protect me from spending unnecessary energy worrying about them. If they had been younger and in better health, they would have come to North Carolina as quickly as possible. Regrettably, long-distance travel was no longer an option, so they had to wait, enduring the hours while they wondered about the fate of their son.

The next call was to Jeff's sister who lived in Orlando. I looked forward to this call because Becky and her husband, Michael, were our spiritual inspiration. Their lives exuded faith and we needed a miracle. Of all the people I knew, Becky and Michael were the most influential and effective ministers of God's power. Involved deeply with jail ministry, almost every conversation we'd had over the years included testimonies of miraculous moves of God restoring people caught in lives of addiction and violence. Becky's powerful, Minnie Pearl-like singing voice and Michael's street-wise preaching style caused even the most hardened criminals to be pierced by the word of God's truth and love. At times incurable diseases had been healed, painful ailments cured, and relationships restored. They both walked with a deep faith and God moved powerfully through them. So I looked forward to this call, in part to inform a family member, but practically, to obtain powerful prayer support.

"Becky, are you in a place where you can sit down?" I asked.

Her response was hesitant. "Yes, what's wrong?" I'm sure she was not expecting to hear my message.

"Your brother is alive, but in the hospital. He's in serious but stable condition. Apparently he's had a heart attack which caused a cardiac arrest." Upon the news she wailed with disbelief. "No!! How could that be?!"

She and Michael had spent vacation time with us just a week prior joining us at the Outer Banks for a couple of days. We had shared many enjoyable moments together and had significant prayers and spiritual conversations. We had left one another with joy, mutually refreshed. That had been exactly one week ago. How could events change so drastically in such a short period of time?

Once Becky recovered her composure she asked what she could do to support us and her brother. Should she come to North Carolina? She could be on her way soon. Since there was nothing to do here but wait, given that Jeff would be in the induced coma at least for another day or two, she decided to stay in Florida, inform remaining family, and spearhead prayer groups on her brother's behalf.

Lastly, I called my own sister, Elizabeth, who lived in the Chicago suburbs with her family. Though she was younger than me by eight years, we had a close relationship. A woman full of good humor and extremely optimistic, Elizabeth took the news with disbelief, another person shocked at the report of Jeff's condition. After making sure my needs were taken care of, she promised to contact our three brothers with the information.

The phone calls complete, I took a deep breath and walked to Jeff's side.

Chapter 11

Saint Francis of Assisi is quoted as saying, "Preach the gospel at all times. If necessary, use words." This "gospel", was preached to me all day Saturday. Friends, neighbors, church members, the home school community, and other individuals changed their own weekend plans and contributed in big and small ways. Some brought coffee, others healthy energy bars. Many offered to keep the boys, or bring them food. Others added our name to prayer chains and communicated Jeff's plight across the country. And those that could made their way to Jeff's bedside to add their voice to the chorus of prayers offered up on his behalf.

One of the Skyland Fire Department paramedics even stopped in to see how Jeff was doing and introduce herself. Whitney was still in awe that Jeff had made it through the ordeal earlier in the day. She was one of the reasons Jeff was still alive, but I found it difficult to find the right words to express my gratitude. So I just hugged her with the request that she pass on my heartfelt thankfulness to the rest of the crew. She assured me she would as she left.

Heroism isn't a word usually associated with hospital visitors, but in some cases it should be. Our neighbor, Hollie, was in a personal struggle with cancer yet willing to stay with me, even to the point of exhaustion. She had seen the ambulance at our house earlier and was one of the first to arrive to the Emergency Room. In and out of hospital rooms herself over the past few months, Hollie should have been resting at home, recovering from her own medical hurdles. Yet she stayed for hours, offering her support. Before fatigue forced her home, Hollie dug into her purse and pulled out a thick roll of one-dollar bills. She thrust them into my hand with the instruction to use them for the little items that I might need, such as snacks or coffee. Hollie's dedication and sacrifice touched me deeply and tears welled up in my eyes as I accepted her gift. Her courage and selflessness were remarkable. Yes, heroic.

Dan and his wife Eva didn't leave the hospital all day, and stayed into the night. They offered support, prayer, and made me eat. They understood my resolve to stay next to Jeff as much as possible. At one point Dan remarked, "Sue, you would take a bullet for Jeff." Standing by a hospital bed in the ICU isn't quite as dramatic as getting shot, but I agreed that I was in this for the long haul.

Rick and Amy stayed with me on and off throughout the day. Friends stopped in to pray for Jeff, then stayed in the waiting room for hours. Jeff's life had touched many, and these were standing with us in our time of need.

Saint Francis would have smiled.

Chapter 12

"Tomorrow morning we've planned something that could very well cause a breakthrough for Jeff."

Tad stood at the foot of Jeff's bed, his eyes gleaming with a combination of excitement and resolve. This was a man of action. Tad rarely stood still and was constantly seeking opportunities to encourage or mentor people in practical ways. If he felt a prompting from God, he acted. This was one of those instances.

"Jeff was dead for 26 minutes," Tad emphasized. "We will ask God to redeem that time and give it back. I've arranged to use the hour before the regular church service to gather together on Jeff's behalf. For 26 minutes we will worship, pray, and read God's word: one minute for each that was taken away. We'll plead on Jeff's behalf and call for God to fully restore him."

Using praise and worship to overcome insurmountable odds is a method God seems to enjoy. The Bible recounts various times God sent musicians and singers before the Israelites in the face of overwhelming opposition only to be victorious. His only request? "Stand firm, hold your position and see the salvation of the Lord."

Passionate in worship himself, Jeff's desire had been to organize people from all around the world in order to sing and worship the Lord at the exact same time. He called it World

Wide Worship. How appropriate to ask for God's favor on Jeff's behalf by using the medium my husband loved the most.

Again, I was humbled by the effort and sacrifice many were exhibiting on Jeff's behalf. But, why not? If any one of these friends were in need, we would do the same for them.

After Tad and Laura prayed for Jeff one last time then left for home, I pondered what they had planned. "Redeem," I thought. "Make an exchange." God had already exchanged life for death. Would he eventually restore everything that may have been lost during those 26 minutes? I felt confident that "26 Minutes of Worship" would have a definite impact in Jeff's favor.

Chapter 13

Sometime that afternoon, our head pastor, Will, returned. This day had thrust him into the emotional highs and lows of being a pastor: coming immediately to the ER to support our family, leaving in order to officiate a wedding, then returning to the Cardiac ICU to check on us again. He was another who stayed for hours, finding out information on my behalf, checking on the boys to make sure they were cared for, sending updates to church members who were asking about us, and generally keeping my focus calm and in perspective.

Will was not only familiar to our church members, but also to the staff of this ICU unit. As is common in many small churches, the pastors hold full-time jobs for a main source of income. Will happened to work for "Life Share", an organization that works alongside families having to make the heart-wrenching decision to remove a loved one from life support, and then accesses permission for organ donation. Time is of the essence in these situations, and a compassionate yet efficient person is needed for this role. At times in the midst of delivering a sermon, Will's pager would sound meaning he was needed to intervene and assist in this delicate family matter.

Though I knew what his position at the hospital entailed, it never entered my mind that perhaps Will might have to come alongside me professionally, not just pastorally. Unknown to me at the time, when Will walked past the nurse's station, one nurse asked him quietly if he was here for the patient in room 357, Jeff's location. He reassured her he was there in the role of pastor, not on Life Share business. Surprise filled her face, not realizing that Will had another job.

Since he was well known to the staff, normally well-kept information about Jeff's condition was passed on to Will. With discretion, he allowed me to hear any positive developments.

He shared that word had spread throughout the Heart Tower, including the Cardiac ICU, of Jeff's tremendous feat of survival. Familiar with his recovery from 26 minutes of CPR, all of the nurses sensed a special quality concerning this particular patient. During quiet moments other nurses from the floor would look in on Jeff and speak encouraging words to me. Other employees had confided they were praying for Jeff. Some had contacted their churches and asked fellow members to pray for his recovery.

Late that night Will was one of my last visitors. He stopped in one last time to see me, encourage me, and reassure me that I was not alone in this struggle.

Chapter 14

As midnight approached, some ladies graciously offered to spend the night with me so I wouldn't be alone, their love for me evident in the sacrifice they were willing to make. I fully appreciated every single visit, prayer, caring word and sentiment shared over the long day and night and did not take any of them for granted. But honestly, I was looking forward to some quiet time to pray, and spend time alone with Jeff. I ushered the last of my friends to the elevators with the promise to call if I needed anything.

As a family, our night time routine has always been to read a passage from the Bible then pray for people we knew who were in need. So it seemed natural to begin reading from the Bible to Jeff. I read out loud until my voice became raspy, then held his cold hand and prayed for those words to sink deep into his being. I thanked God for what he was doing in our crisis and for his faithfulness to our family. I asked again for a miracle, reminding myself that "nothing is impossible with God."

By now it was after 2:00 a.m. and I'd been up for almost 20 hours. I knew the next day would be full of activity and visitors so felt I should try to get sleep if even for a couple of hours. Though it was a struggle to leave Jeff's side for more than a few minutes, I knew the nurses were attending to his every physical need. So I found a blanket and my pillow, took off my shoes, and laid down on the couch in the waiting room. I turned off the light.

Closing my eyes and trying to relax, I was suddenly overwhelmed with a smothering and heart-pounding fear. Faith was replaced with a palpable dread. My heart began beating faster, my breaths short and shallow, my thoughts almost paralyzed. My mind was filled with the awful thought that Jeff would die and we would be alone.

Sitting up, gulping in breaths, I tried to get ahold of my rampaging emotions. Why oh, why did I think I'd be fine by myself alone all night? *"God has not given us a spirit of fear, but of love, discipline, and a sound mind."* That scripture, found in the second book of Timothy, came subtly but firmly to my mind. As I thought about that verse, I regained my conviction.

"God, you have not given me a spirit of fear, but of love, discipline, and a sound mind," I firmly recited.

Recognizing my terror was unfounded, I forced myself to think of what I knew to be true, not trusting my imagination. "My hope and trust is in the Lord," I spoke into the night. "God, it is *you* who holds every day of Jeff's life in your hands. Every day has been ordained by *you*, God, and I trust that when Jeff's days are through on this earth, whether today, tomorrow or in 50 years, that it will be *your* perfect timing. So I don't need to be afraid!"

I reminded myself of the words of the worship songs I played in Jeff's room just a short time before: *"Our God is fighting for us always... our God is fighting for us now. We are not alone..... We are not alone..."*

37

And, *"You give life. You are love. You bring light to the darkness. You give hope. You restore. Great are you Lord!"*

Refocused, I lay back down and slept.

Chapter 15

Sunday: Father's Day

My watch showed 5:00 a.m. and aside from the quietness of the hallway, all was the same as when I curled up on the small couch in the family waiting room three hours earlier. I pushed the buzzer for after-hours admittance to the ICU and the doors swung open. The nurses at the station smiled politely as I entered and walked to Jeff's bed. Nothing seemed to have changed: Jeff was just as still as ever, the breathing machine giving him life. All of the monitors showed that his pulse, blood pressure, and oxygen level were just fine. His body temperature continued to hover at 91 degrees, the Arctic Sun doing its job.

I did my best to stay out of their way as Jeff's nurses gave him constant care by checking his vital signs, cleaning him, making sure his blankets were on, and adjusting anything amiss. My respect for them continued to increase as I watched their dedication and professionalism. One nurse, 8 months pregnant, toiled energetically through work that I knew must have been exhausting. She was already 10 hours into her 12-hour shift.

When they left to care for another patient, I took my usual position by Jeff's side and picked up his hand. Leaning close to his cheek I spoke to my husband, prayed for him, and recounted what Tad had planned later that morning at our church. Then I turned and rebooted the computer. I found some nice worship music and songs about God's majesty filled the little space.

Opening my Bible and laying it on the bed I turned to the book of Psalms, right in the middle. These songs and poems were written to urge people to come to God in any and every circumstance. Some are reminders that God is majestic, others to praise him with thanksgiving and joy. The bulk of the passages in the Psalms, however, are filled with prayers and pleas to God on behalf of the authors caught in dangerous, heartbreaking, or life-threatening circumstances.

Before this day I would relate to those particular writings much as I would a fictional novel: on the outside looking in on an emotional situation. The writers were putting forth their predicaments, expressing emotion, asking God for his intervention then praising him for his grandeur and holiness, regardless if he delivered them or not.

Yes, our family had experienced troubles. We'd had a chimney fire years before, the death of my parents, financial struggles here and there, and even some major medical challenges. What we were facing now was an entirely different level of crisis. For once I could identify with the raw emotions the poets of Psalms laid out. I wasn't reading these poems and songs as a dispassionate reader, but as a real person needing reassurance that God was involved and moving in my situation. I was looking for God's promise for me. With 150 Psalms, where was I to begin?

"God," I prayed, "show me your promises. I really need your touch this morning."

As I turned the pages and read, each one seemed to perfectly answer my deepest longings for my husband, lying comatose before me. The thoughts and words and promises seemed to spill off the pages of my Bible into my being. It seemed that God was speaking directly to me, to again remind me that I was not alone, that he was involved and taking care of Jeff. He had answered my simple prayer for guidance.

Psalm 20: 1,2, 4-5, 7 (ESV) *May the Lord answer you in the day of trouble! May he send you help from the sanctuary... May he grant you your heart's desire and fulfill all your plans! May we shout for joy over your salvation, and in the name of our God set up our banners! May the Lord fulfill all your petitions! Some trust in chariots and some in horses, but we will trust in the name of the Lord our God.*

Psalm 91: 2, 15-16 (ESV) *I will say to the Lord, "My refuge and my fortress, my God in whom I trust"...I (God) will be with him in trouble; I will rescue him and honor him...With long life I will satisfy him and show him my salvation.*

Psalm 41: 1-3 (ESV) *Blessed is the one who considers the poor! In the day of trouble the Lord delivers him; the Lord protects him and keeps him alive...The Lord sustains him on his sickbed; in his illness you restore him to full health.*

As I read on I couldn't contain my excitement. These words weren't just nice, they were perfect. Each one was exactly what I needed to focus on. It would have taken me hours to have found these verses on my own. It was as if God himself had focused my attention on the precise words he wanted to show me. I couldn't have chosen better scriptures to encourage me and refresh my spirit. The Lord's personal commitment to me was overwhelming. Feeling God's peace and assurance I felt ready to face the rest of the day.

Chapter 16

It wasn't long before various medical staff came to check Jeff's early morning status. Some were technicians, others specialists. Most came in, checked his chart, and moved on to the other patients on their list. They all had a long day ahead of them and Jeff was just one of a multitude on their roster.

The nurses seemed to show a great deal of respect for the next doctor to walk in. Wearing a business suit under a white lab coat, the doctor introduced himself as Jeff's cardiologist, Dr. William Hathaway. "The doctor normally assigned to the ICU today couldn't make it in, so I am filling in for him. I'll take care of your husband as long as he's in the hospital," Dr. Hathaway explained.

After asking me many of the same questions about Jeff's health history that I answered yesterday he shared some basic thoughts. "His numbers look good," the doctor said. "It's a great sign that he's made it through the night." After hearing that news, I felt a bit of relief and optimism for Jeff's survival and recovery.

"We still don't have the results of his bloodwork, which will probably reveal what is amiss in his system. I think a heart attack is the most likely culprit behind his cardiac arrest. It is quite lucky that he is still alive."

Never knowing how some people respond to people of faith, I felt compelled to explain: "There are a lot of people praying for Jeff. We are all standing in faith that God will make something good out of this."

The cardiologist regarded me and thought of the words I had just shared. After a moment he replied, "I will join you in that."

Grateful for yet another in the medical realm that had offered to come along side us in faith, I felt a type of peace and joy despite the strain that comes from waiting.

After he moved on, Jeff's head nurse confided that he was not only the best cardiologist in the hospital but also the Chief Medical Officer. It struck me that it was no accident this man happened to fill in for the usual cardiologist. I marveled anew at the way God was placing just the right nurses and medical staff around Jeff. From among the earliest prayers on Jeff's behalf one specific appeal was for God to choose the doctors and nurses that would be assigned to his care. Convinced this was the case, I knew God would use Dr. Hathaway to help Jeff.

Chapter 17

The morning also brought back visitors. At first I was uncomfortably aware when more than two people were standing in the cramped space when the stated limit was two. Shortly after 7:00 a.m., Tad and Laura, then Dan and Eva stopped in to see how Jeff made it through the night. Soon Rick and Amy dropped by on their way to the church. The nurses were almost complete with their shift turnover, and I relaxed when they didn't seem upset about the number of my visitors. I was glad to have these as my early morning support group. As I looked into their faces I knew that they had not slept much either. Jeff was their good friend, too. Losing him would be like losing a blood brother. My pain was also their pain. The term "church family" was absolutely appropriate.

Then I asked a favor, an idea that had been forming all morning. "Could you ask if any of the worship team would be willing to come and sing here in Jeff's room?" I was aware it was Father's Day and people would have planned dinners and gatherings with family. I didn't want to intrude on that special time, but I knew that live worship music holds a certain power that can't come across through the speakers of a laptop computer. *"God inhabits the praises of his people"*, was another familiar Bible passage to me. Oh, how wonderful it would be to invite God's presence through live music into Jeff's room later in the day!

With a promise to pass on that request, the group left for our church.

As 9:30 a.m. drew near, I suspected more dear friends and church members were gathering at Gateway to pray on Jeff's behalf. "26 Minutes of Worship." I tried to imagine what may be happening during that time. Tad would lay out the need, explain the purpose, and then begin. It would be a no-nonsense time to worship then pray for a loved and needful friend. Consisting of acoustic and electric guitar, bass, drum set, and vocalists, our church worship is not a show or performance, but a deep offering to the one worthy of all praise. I knew there would be much heartfelt involvement from all who participated.

One of my greatest joys is to watch Jeff worship. He closes his eyes and loses himself in the music and the words, almost as if he's in another place. At this moment, miles from our church sanctuary, I prayed that he would be able to sense the music that was playing three feet away. I chose several songs that my son Josh had included and began my own 26 minutes of worship.

Before long, my thoughts were removed from our situation and focused upon God and his might. Some songs spoke of God's holiness, his presence in all situations, and his strength. Others exclaimed that God is a mighty tower and shelter; we can come to him for strength and protection. They reminded me that I can sing to the Lord from the time the sun comes up until it sets no matter my circumstances. God was and is and always will be worthy of my worship.

Transitioning, I focused on songs that conveyed my desperation for God. Lyrics affirmed that I can be sure His love remains; it never gives up on me. His love is stronger than the power of the grave. His love is constant through the trials we face. Another song declared he's the God who conquers giants, he's the God who shut the mouths of lions and the one that caused the dead to breathe. I can always depend upon him.

Before I knew it, an hour had passed by. Sensing that God was in the midst of the prayers and petitions of his people here in the hospital, a few miles away at Gateway, and in other parts of the country perhaps, I couldn't help but wonder at the peace and calm I felt. The atmosphere was hopeful.

By now I knew the prayer time would have finished and the congregation at Gateway was preparing for the usual church service. I reflected on how vital my circle of friends had been to me and the boys. Then I took time to thank God specifically for the wonderful people we had in our lives.

Chapter 18

Shortly after noon, Dr. Hathaway returned. "The blood work came back on your husband. He definitely had a heart attack. There are enzymes created by the body that are only produced during a heart attack, so I am confident of this diagnosis," he carefully explained.

As I sat back deeper in my chair, the doctor must have seen the perplexed look on my face.

"You say he hasn't had any symptoms of heart trouble and no history in his family?" he inquired again.

"None," I said. "What will you do now?"

Dr. Hathaway scrutinized me. I wasn't the kind of wife that was falling apart with each piece of bad news, so he went on, trusting my disposition would continue.

"Jeff's temperature has been at 91 degrees for the necessary 24 hours. We will slowly bring his temperature up to normal. Then we will go from there. We don't know the damage that may have been caused by the cardiac arrest. Twenty-six minutes is a long time for the brain to go without fully oxygenated blood. The neurologist will give his input after reading the brain scans. Then in due time, we'll check for heart damage from the heart attack. For now, we'll wait."

Not sure if he had been informed of my three hours of rest or if he was just a good judge of character, I listened as he continued on as a concerned physician: "Mrs. Lyons, keep in mind that this is not a sprint, but a marathon. Your husband may be here awhile. Take care of yourself and get some rest." With a nod, he left.

Despite my faith, and though God had proven his involvement in this dire situation, I still had moments of wavering. This was one of them. The doctor seemed convinced there would be damage to Jeff's heart. Though he didn't speak the words out loud, he had alluded to a real possibility that Jeff would have brain damage. Was there the possibility he would never come out of the coma? Was there something being discerned through the brain waves transmitted on the monitor that he understood but was keeping from me for now? Once again I felt my resolve ebbing.

"This is not a sprint, but a marathon," the doctor had emphasized. The release date written on the white board: "30 days", was a constant reminder that the doctors indeed had a prognosis and it wasn't for a miraculous healing. A long, drawn-out recovery, perhaps, but not a supernatural sweep of God's power.

My mind was assaulted with images from true stories of families devastated by traumatic brain damage. One husband's personality had been completely changed; he didn't even recognize his own wife when he woke from a coma. A son needed nursing care for the rest of his life.

My heart was gripped with anguish. At once, I wondered if it might have been better if Jeff had died. Will the rest of his life on earth bring grief to our family? If he wakes up, will he even recognize me? Will he be the same Jeff or will we have to contend with a "stranger"? Am I prepared to be his caregiver for the rest of his life, if he isn't able to perform daily tasks? What if he remains in a vegetative state? These frightening and sobering possibilities assaulted my thoughts.

The question I really needed to answer was: "God, can I trust you with Jeff's life, no matter what?"

I forced myself to refocus my thoughts. What could be the worst case scenario? Jeff would die and be forever in God's presence never to suffer again. The sorrow would be for us, not him. What if he survived but needed extended nursing care? Then the boys and I would learn to trust God and lean on one another as we worked through the loss and the grief. Would God forsake us? Never. Would he leave us to fend for ourselves? Absolutely not.

Looking at the brain waves on the monitor I gave Jeff's life and situation back to God.

Chapter 19

Remembering that I had asked some of our worship team to visit and sing for Jeff, I'd forgotten to ask the nurse if it would be all right.   Not wanting to take advantage of her kindness and assume a favorable response, I broached the subject. Valerie regarded my request and as gently as she could, reminded me of the visitation limit of two people. Recognizing our group had been exceeding that number for 24 hours, it was time to respect the needs of the hospital staff to most effectively fulfill their jobs. I reminded myself that God is not limited by numbers, and not to fret.

At 2:00 in the afternoon the boys, along with some of our closest friends joined me at Jeff's bedside. Sam, Josh, and Micah walked up to their dad and spoke loving words to him. Rick and Amy gave me homemade cards that three little girls from one family had made for Jeff. The bright crayon drawings showed a stick man Jeff standing up holding the hands of his stick-man family. All had red crayon smiles. "I love you, Mr. Jeff" was lettered as carefully as their little hands could manage. I set up the three cards on his bedside table. Simple childlike faith reminded me of how God asks us to come to him.

The nurses stepped in to care for some of Jeff's needs. Their job would be easier with some elbow room, so I took the opportunity to show my gratefulness to those that had come to visit and pray. As I exited the ICU and walked toward the waiting room I had been using, a lighthearted atmosphere prevailed. All who were there had a cheerfulness about them. This was not a crowd expecting terrible news but hopeful for a good report. They had all turned a corner in the way they were praying for Jeff and waited to see how long it would be until God answered their heartfelt prayers.

Word was relayed to me about the "26 Minutes of Worship." It was no surprise that 26 minutes was not enough to contain the prayers, petitions, and pleas on behalf of a beloved friend and Christian brother. They shared that as the music began, the crowd responded. The words to the songs were sung with passion and conviction. Faces were turned toward heaven, hands lifted high. The music faded, then one by one people stood and spoke scriptures and prayers out loud for Jeff. Twenty-six minutes came and went; no one was leaving. More people came into the sanctuary. Almost everyone was aware of Jeff's crisis and they had come to stand for him before the Creator of life.

Old, young, parents, grandparents, young adults, teens, and in some cases entire families came to participate. My three boys were part of the group. Some clasped hands under their chins, silently lifting up their heartfelt entreaties. Others were on their knees. Still more lying face down, heaving with sobs emanating from deep in their souls. They were meeting with their God, asking for life, pleading for healing. They were of one mind, one heart, and one focus. Jeff and Jeff's healing and restoration was the only thing on their minds.

Humbled and grateful, I basked in the description of what had transpired that morning. Again I was uplifted and encouraged. God was loving me and our family deeply. I was amazed again at people's commitment to us and love for us. Following Dr. Hathaway's advice, I waited. But I was waiting with hope.

Chapter 20

Dan, Eva, and I were standing by Jeff's bed, having a quiet and meaningful conversation when we were aware of nursing staff rushing to the room next to us. A doctor whisked by. Suddenly, the air was pierced with a heart-wrenching wail followed by loud sobs. A patient had died.

Shortly thereafter chaos ensued. One of the teenage daughters was beside herself with grief. She was shouting and screaming for her father to come back. Another family member was yelling at the nurses, cursing them for letting him die.

Nurses and other staff were doing their best to calm the situation and bring order to the ICU floor. Already under strain caring for critically ill patients, the nurses were professional and calm in the face of yet another crisis. My respect for them and their abilities increased even more.

It wasn't long before a hospital security guard escorted the family out of the ICU into the hallway. The daughter was weeping hysterically, screaming for "Daddy". My heart was breaking for her. Retreating to the hallway, I quietly shared with our group what had happened.

By now Sam and Josh had arrived to take part in the worship time in Jeff's room. I explained to them that this family needed to experience God's peace and strength, too. They were overcome with grief and didn't appear to have any semblance of peace or faith to help them face this tragedy. This family had lost a beloved relative. Perhaps we were here to offer the prayers they desperately needed.

Together we prayed for this family and asked for God to extend his comfort into their lives. I stood by in my silent vigil on their behalf. The man who had cursed the doctor and nurses stomped away still enraged, but simmering instead of explosive.

More family members came to mourn and weep together. The girl's sobbing, though punctuated with loud wails, began to subside. A motherly woman enveloped this suffering girl in arms of love and I heard her praying to "Dear Jesus", with calm and reassurance. I sensed peace beginning to descend on the group.

Though sad for this family, I hoped their strong family bond would help them carry on.

Chapter 21

While the grieving family still filled the hallway, the worship team arrived. Patrick was one of the men who had retrieved the boys the day before. As the leader of the worship team, he had a deep and caring nature. Alex also helped lead our team and had brought his guitar. Both men, aside from loving music and worship, also had the quality of a tender spirit. Rick and Amy, along with their daughters Kendra and Diana, rounded out the group.

Breaking the news that the nurse would only allow two in the room, the team agreed Patrick and Alex would be the best choices. Josh decided Sam would be the family member represented since he also had a deep love of worship. As I led the group toward Jeff's spot I explained to Alex that it was likely the nurse wouldn't allow the guitar due to the restricted space surrounding Jeff's bed.

We all filed quietly into Jeff's area. The nurse was adjusting Jeff's position and I reminded Valerie that we'd come to sing for Jeff. I introduced Sam, my son, then Alex and Patrick.

With a soft voice, Alex humbly asked Valerie if he could use his guitar. She said that would be fine.

"I'll try my best to be quiet as I play and sing," he spoke. "I understand your concerns."

Valerie had a smile on her face when she said "Well, be sure to play and sing loud enough that I can join in!" Perhaps the ruckus of an hour ago had put some quiet music into a different perspective.

My heart leapt again! She wasn't flinching that four of us were with Jeff. My heart's desire was for Josh to take part in this time as well, so I rushed back to the waiting room and encouraged him to take my place. Josh eagerly went, glad to be able to be a part of this unusual but valuable time. And as I watched him enter the ICU, heading to Jeff's side, I rejoiced and thanked God yet again for working out the small details that were mounting up as the hours progressed.

Chapter 22

While the four were in Jeff's room, I was suddenly aware of two women in the adjoining waiting room. When I'd come here to sleep at 2:00 a.m. that room had been dark, the door closed. During the daytime I'd walked past and noticed a pillow, blanket, and jacket. A couple of times I'd seen the two ladies napping, obviously tired and uncomfortable. As my friends chatted and waited, I stepped into their waiting room and introduced myself. These two were from out of town, their father in very serious condition.

As they shared about their father's plight and resolve to stay with him as long as he was in the ICU, I thought of the contrast between my situation and theirs. Yesterday, I had felt alone but was soon surrounded by a multitude of friends. These two really were alone; no friends were coming and their father was hanging precariously to life. My heart was filled with compassion. I hugged them tightly, connected by a similar thread of need and struggle.

"Please, if you need anything, I'll help if I can," I offered.

Tears in their eyes, their sole request was prayer for their father. Sincere love is void of selfishness, wanting only the best for others. These precious daughters were yearning for their father to be well and at peace. They were exhibiting love in the purest sense.

Yes, of course I would pray. At that very moment I grasped their hands, bowed my head, and appealed to God. I asked for the Father of the world to wrap his arms of love and strength around these weary daughters. I asked for his peace to quiet their hearts. I prayed that his promises would comfort and be a source of security for them during their moments of insecurity. And above all, I asked that his healing would extend to their father.

There was not a dry eye in that little room when we were done. And for good reason. There is something emotional and powerful that occurs when Heaven meets Earth. It is cleansing to know that tears and trust can be compatible. Weariness can be lifted when the burden is shared and though in some ways I was a stranger to these ladies, our common struggle gave us a connection that can only be realized in the midst of tragedy.

Chapter 23

At 6:00 p.m., almost a half hour from when they began, the four returned to the waiting room. I couldn't help but notice the excitement revealed on all of their faces.

Sam began, "After we started singing, the room was filled with such a feeling of peace. We could all feel it," he expressed, still in awe of what had happened. "I felt like we weren't just worshipping, but we were doing something. It was making a difference."

The rest of the group nodded in agreement.

"I've never felt anything like it," Alex marveled. He spoke to all of us gathered, "I have to admit that my first reaction was fear. I haven't been around anyone that appeared the way Jeff did lying there in that hospital bed." Alex's honesty spoke to me of the courage it took for him to stay in the room, uncomfortable yet obedient to my wishes and willing to put Jeff's needs before his own fear. My throat tightened with emotion.

He went on. "We started by singing, '*Let it rain…open the floodgates of Heaven.*' We followed that with a chorus that says '*Come just like you promised, just like you said you would.*'" He took a deep breath then continued, "Because as we were standing there it became so evident how much we *needed* him to come.

"When we were done singing, the fear in that room was gone. The thing that remained was God's peace. God's peace flooded that room," Alex finished.

Even my quiet, contemplative son, Josh, had a joyful and peaceful countenance. Heaven had once again met Earth. God confirmed that he was in the midst of our crisis. Worship made a difference. Peace overcame fear. Thirty minutes in the Cardiac Intensive Care Unit helped all of us turn a corner.

Since it was Father's Day, everyone gathered their things to go home to celebrate. Grateful that they had taken time away from their families to honor my request on Jeff's behalf, I walked them to the elevators. Rick and Amy would host a houseful with three generations coming to share a meal. My own sons would spend the evening with good friends that lived a mere three miles from the hospital.

I was in no way downcast by the reality that our family would not be celebrating in the usual way. God the Father had been showing his love toward us in many ways in the past two days. I returned to Jeff's bedside and held his hand, gazing at his face. His hand was no longer cold, his body temperature rising with each hour. Despite my roller coaster emotions, I was hopeful.

"Thank you, God," I began to pray. "Thank you for the 18 years you've given to us. No matter what happens, I'll thank you for whatever is ahead of us as well."

As I thought of Jeff's role as a father, and the positive impact he'd had on our three sons, I continued: "Praise you for the wonderful father you allowed Jeff to be for Sam, Josh, and

Micah. You instilled within him a deep responsibility to be the best father possible, and he has been. Thank you."

I reflected on a well-known Lyons family story. One of Jeff's humorous quotes from childhood was, "When I grow up, I want to be a big daddy and drive a big car!" Jeff was a great father, his dream from childhood realized three times over. Not long ago, when asked who his hero was, Josh admitted, "My dad, because he loves God and is the wisest man I know." What greater compliment could a teenage boy give his father?

No, we would not be celebrating Father's Day in the usual manner. But I could still celebrate my husband and his role as the best father I could ever have imagined for my children.

Chapter 24

It was 6:30 p.m. and Valerie's shift was coming to a close. She had been a great source of comfort and encouragement throughout the day. I was grateful for her and the part she had in caring for Jeff.

Glancing at one of the monitors she said, "Your husband's body temperature is up. Once we make the switchover, your night nurse will take the next steps." I made a mental note of the time. It had only been a half hour since the worship team had left Jeff's side. Just 15 minutes ago, I'd said good-bye to my sons, expecting to see them in the morning.

An overlap of 30 minutes is used as the day nurse passes on vital information to the night nurse. This sharing of information is critical and taken seriously by each. I watched as Kendall meticulously wrote down details on her charts and notebooks. She was the nurse eight months pregnant, beginning her second night in a row caring for Jeff.

Kendall shared with me that since she was the nurse overseeing the Cardiac ICU tonight, Jeff was her only patient. So far tonight, there weren't very many patients, though that could change quickly. Therefore, she could give him much of her time and attention.

Another young woman slipped into the space, short of stature and with a bubbly personality. She pulled up a stool next to Jeff opposite where I was sitting and holding his hand. With a smile she introduced herself. "I'm Maureen, a respiratory therapist."

Kendall explained that Jeff's body temperature was back to normal so it was time to halt the paralyzing and sedating drugs being administered to him by IV. She reached up and put a clip in a tube leading to one of Jeff's arms which stopped the flow. It was 7:15 p.m.

"For someone like your husband, who has been on the Arctic Sun, we usually don't get a response for at least 24 to 48 hours. We'll maintain constant surveillance on him since he'll struggle with the breathing tube when he rouses. There will always be a respiratory therapist close by to monitor Jeff's breathing. Then, at an appropriate time, a neurologist will interpret the brain waves and see what impact the trauma of the cardiac arrest has had on his brain function."

"Every patient is different," she added. "We're really hoping for good results with Jeff. He's been through a lot but we also know he's tough or he wouldn't be with us."

I glanced nervously again at the monitor showing the brain activity. My promise to stay with Jeff in sickness and in health came to my mind as I silently prayed for him.

The atmosphere was relaxed. We talked about little things. Kendall and her husband would be painting and decorating the baby's room on her days off. Maureen loved her job and spent her days off hiking and enjoying the mountains.

My attention was drawn to Jeff's face. His breaths were steady, his body still.

Then I noticed a slight movement as his eyes stirred beneath the closed lids. His lip twitched.

"He's moving!" I exclaimed. "Is he waking up?" Hadn't Kendall just said that it usually takes 24 to 48 hours for a patient to revive after being on the Arctic Sun? Transfixed, I couldn't take my eyes off of him.

Both women stopped in mid-sentence and gave their attention to Jeff. Sure enough he was moving! His head rocked back and forth and his eyes struggled to open. Suddenly he began resisting the breathing tube in his throat, gagging violently. His eyes opened and a look of panic filled his face.

Kendall stood and took charge. "Mr. Lyons!" she commanded loudly and clearly. Her eyes grew wide as Jeff turned his head and looked directly at her, continuing to fight the breathing tube.

"You are in the hospital and that tube is helping you to breathe. Try to relax and let it work for you," Kendall instructed. Jeff followed her directions and his anxiety eased slightly.

Maureen's face showed shock, wonder, and amazement at what she was witnessing. She, too, stood to her feet, unable to sit still. Jeff was noticeably groggy, but aware of his surroundings.

"Mr. Lyons…can you squeeze my hand?" Kendall asked as she held Jeff's right hand. I watched as his fingers moved one at a time, slowly, but methodically as he put pressure on hers. "Now, can you squeeze my other hand?" She reached over and held his left hand. Again, he responded to her request.

She lifted the blankets off his feet. "Now, Mr. Lyons, can you move your feet and toes?" All of us watched as we saw his feet move slowly but deliberately. His toes spread apart then bent. He pressed his feet against Kendall's hands.

I found myself speechless. Glancing at one of the ICU monitors I noted it was 7:35 p.m. The drugs had been stopped a mere 20 minutes earlier. Jeff wasn't expected to show any signs of awareness for at least a day or more, yet here he was, following Kendall's every instruction. Hadn't Sam marveled that he and the worship team had felt something change in the atmosphere of this room? That their worship was actually making a difference?

Maureen turned to me and spoke with deep emotion, "Mrs. Lyons, you call those boys of yours and tell them their daddy is going to be OK."

Kendall agreed. "Yes! Go ahead and make that call!"

I didn't need to be convinced! I picked up my cell phone and punched in the number for our friends. Sam answered, recognizing my number. "Hi, Mom," he answered with a bit of trepidation in his voice.

"Sam! I've got good news! Dad is awake and he's following the instructions the nurses are giving him!" I could hardly contain my excitement. I looked at both Kendall and Maureen, trying to get their opinion as I continued, "I don't think it's an exaggeration to say it's a miracle!"

Both women looked at me and vigorously nodded in agreement.

"Yes! It *is* a miracle," Maureen emphasized.

"So, Sam, tell your brothers. Dad is going to be OK!"

"Thanks, Mom! That's great news! Tell Dad we love him," Sam said with thick emotion in his voice.

After hanging up I needed to make one more call.

"Rick! I know you are in the middle of your Father's Day supper right now, but I don't think you'll mind being interrupted with this news… Jeff is awake! And he's following instructions from the nurses! It's a miracle!!"

What a contrast to the phone call he and Amy received from me the morning before. Again, there was a moment of silence, but a loud "whoop" followed this message. After hanging up I could only imagine the joy they were sharing around that dinner table!

Chapter 25

There is a protocol for everything medical. The Pulmonary Specialist had to check Jeff and remove his breathing tube. However, she wouldn't be in until the early morning so Jeff was sedated once more.

He would be aroused at 3:00 a.m. for one hour to establish his readiness for the removal of the breathing tube. The nurses warned that it would be a difficult time for him. When awake and alert it is very difficult to handle a breathing tube. The "gag reflex" would cause Jeff's body to react to the large, plastic tube protruding down his throat.

Their attention would be on keeping him calm and distracted until that hour was completed.

In the meantime, I had phone calls to make! This time, it was a joy to relate the good news. Now my phone calls had an encouraging purpose. One by one I called family. First Jeff's parents, then my sister. Overjoyed reactions at the other end of the phone line assaulted my ears, but I didn't mind.

I saved the phone call to Becky, Jeff's sister, for last.

"Becky! I've got great news! The nurses brought your brother out of the coma and he was able to understand their instructions! He even looked them in the eye when they called his name. "

"What?!" she said with a sense of wonder and elation in her voice.

I shared with her the events of the evening including Sam and Josh taking part in the worship time in Jeff's room just two hours ago.

"No way! What time exactly?" she asked with a measure of excitement in her voice.

I knew I was about to hear something amazing. When I told her it was from about 5:30 to 6:00 she said, "You're not going to believe this. But why not? God does this sort of thing all the time!

"Every Sunday night I've been leading a worship service at a church called "Voice of Healing". Tonight I was upset and told the group that I needed prayer for my brother. Everyone could tell this was really serious. We started singing and worshipping at 5:15 and God's presence was so powerful! I felt filled with God's spirit and was proclaiming a supernatural healing move of God on Jeff's body. We finished at 6:00, so for most of that time we were praying and worshipping at the exact time as you were."

She added thoughtfully, "I really wanted to drive up immediately to be with you, but I felt God wanted me to stay here. Now I know why." Becky laughed with joy and a deep emotional release. "God... you are awesome!" she exclaimed.

When I hung up after speaking with Becky, and before I had a chance to digest what God had done through her overlapping worship service, Amy and her daughter Diana came rushing up. Though in the midst of their meal just minutes before, they came to the hospital to rejoice in the miracle God had performed. Rick, Patrick, and Kendra followed a few minutes later.

For the time being, neither the nurses nor I were bothered by the breaching of the two-person limit around Jeff's bed. There was an atmosphere of celebration that rarely occurs in this part of the hospital. We all looked with a sense of wonder at Jeff, asleep again.

Rick laughed as he said, "After you called, and I shared the news to everyone gathered at our house, we put down our forks and pulled out our phones! In a matter of minutes your news spread like wildfire throughout the church body. This is a time to thank God for the great things he has done."

I agreed wholeheartedly with Rick. We all circled around Jeff's bed and spent time thanking God for the great miracle that he had performed.

That night as I lay down on the waiting room couch, I wasn't contending with fear, but expectation.

Chapter 26

Monday:

I got up at 2:30 a.m. Not wanting to miss Jeff's next awakening, I had slept lightly. As I stepped out into the quiet hallway, I noticed the lights were off in the waiting room of the two daughters. Speaking a silent prayer on their behalf, I asked God to give them refreshing rest, and healing for their father.

The doors to the Cardiac ICU swung open for me and I made my way through the now familiar route to Jeff's bedside. Kendall and Maureen were preparing for the next crucial step.

They both concurred that this is usually the most difficult part of the transition for the patient, but absolutely necessary. The purpose was to ascertain if Jeff's body was ready to breathe on its own without the aid of a breathing tube. They would have to take him off of sedation. The forced oxygen would be halted and the nurses would watch to see if Jeff could breathe independently for a full hour.

They conceded that brain damage can interrupt the body's ability to function naturally. If he couldn't breathe normally, it could be a sign of damage, though not necessarily. In that case they would again put him under and wait for a neurologist to run tests. But if independent breathing was successful, the morning pulmonologist would remove the tube, a big step toward improvement.

Both Kendall and Maureen wanted to make sure I was prepared for Jeff's struggle. "He will writhe and fight the tube. Will you be all right with that? If not, you can go back to your waiting room and we'll get you when we're done. This can be terribly upsetting."

Though I appreciated their concern, I felt able to handle almost anything and wanted to be a part of keeping my husband calm in the midst of a troubling experience. For better or for worse, right? What could be worse than panic? What could be better than support? I was ready.

Kendall reached up and put a clip in the IV line that was delivering the sedation to Jeff's body. Now we were prepared for Jeff movements after witnessing his response the evening before.

Just as expected, when Jeff revived, he fought against the breathing tube. His body almost lifted out of his bed as he reacted to the tube in his throat, gagging, panic on his face. Once again, Kendall spoke to Jeff. "Mr. Lyons. You are in the hospital. The tube is helping you to breathe. Let it do its job."

Holding tight to his hand, I stood and leaned toward his face. "Honey, I'm here." Jeff turned toward me, trying to understand. For the first time in more than two days my husband was looking at me. "Try to relax. The tube in your throat is helping you breath. I love you, Honey. Relax." I wasn't exactly sure how often to repeat those words, I did know that his panic ebbed and he seemed able to handle the tube. I also wasn't sure if he recognized me or if he was just responding to the voice of another person giving him directions.

Kendall continued with her instructions. Once again she asked Jeff to squeeze her hands and move his feet. Then she increased the difficulty by asking him to lift his arms and legs. He nodded to the question if he knew his name. He shook his head when asked if he knew why he was in the hospital.

Each function and every correct answer brought encouragement to all of us.

Then they explained that they would turn off the forced air.

Once this was done, Maureen asked, "Mr. Lyons, can you take a deep breath for me?"

He did. Jeff no longer struggled against the tube in his throat. He appeared relaxed and ready to follow the nurses' instructions. He continued breathing without the aid of the machines. His situation was looking more optimistic with each hurdle he successfully maneuvered.

Between the three of us, we managed to keep Jeff distracted enough that the hour passed by without incident. It was good news. Jeff was capable of breathing on his own. Maureen even suggested with enthusiasm that if the Pulmonary Specialist could arrive now, Jeff could have the tube removed immediately.

My eyebrows raised questioningly.

"I'm only a technician," Maureen explained. "A Pulmonary Specialist has the training to discern whether a patient is ready to have a breathing tube removed."

However, even though the specialist did come early, it would still be hours before that could happen. Jeff was tranquilized one last time while we waited for the specialist to arrive.

I started some praise and worship music. Elated, I listened to the same words to the same songs with gratefulness. Yesterday I had played the music as a prayer request; it was a way to keep my mind focused on God's mercies and power. Today my thoughts were filled with relief, expectation, and hope.

Told of Jeff's recovery, the Pulmonary Specialist made him the first stop of her day. The routine was repeated: Jeff's sedation was stopped and he revived. The oxygen was stopped and Jeff was asked to breath on his own. Satisfied, the doctor prepared to remove the tube, and I was surprised that it only took a minute.

The next step was one of the worst. Unknown to me, fluids build up in the lungs when intubated; these can be life threatening if not removed, causing pneumonia or worse.

"He is not going to like this," the pulmonologist stated calmly, "but it has to be done."

She turned on suction and began removing the liquids from his lungs. Jeff writhed, wretched, and struggled. It seemed to take a long time, but in reality was accomplished in only about two minutes. "Fortunately, he won't remember a thing," the pulmonologist explained. "Some of his medications have the side effect of minor amnesia, which is a good benefit in this case." She gave me a reassuring smile. "He did great!" she said on her way out.

His eyes were open and roving the room as Jeff seemed to be assessing his situation. Already the trauma of a moment ago seemed to be forgotten.

Now the nurses moved in to make Jeff comfortable as an alert patient. They elevated his bed, fluffed his pillows, and spoke to him. "Mr. Lyons, are you thirsty?" After a nod, I watched, still in awe, as Kendall held up a cup of ice water to his lips and Jeff took a sip through the plastic straw. How can such a basic skill seem so miraculous? As for me, I would marvel at the return of everyday functions for many days to come.

Chapter 27

The nurses left and it was only the two of us, together. I held Jeff's hand and gazed into his eyes. Even though he had just recently awakened, he had already proven he could understand instructions and respond to perfect strangers. For more than 40 hours I had watched the brain waves on the monitor. Doctor Hathaway had tried to prepare me for the worst. "Release date: 30 days" was still written in marker on the whiteboard. I just had to know…

"Do you know who I am?" I tentatively asked.

Jeff's eyes rested on my face. He was quiet for just a moment, then tenderly shared with a smile, "You're my wife." His voice was deep and hoarse from the breathing tube, but it was Jeff's.

My heart leapt. My tense muscles relaxed as my greatest fear was absolved. The long, dark hours of wondering if he would ever wake up, then if he would remember me or his past life were summed up in his short and concise answer. He was awake! He knew who I was. My husband was on the road to recovery.

His head rested on the pillow. Jeff glanced both ways, then at me as if getting ready to share a secret.

"Where am I?" he whispered.

I wasn't surprised at this question. He had just awakened after almost 48 hours in a coma. Lying on a hospital bed and surrounded by medical equipment must have been shocking.

"You are in the Cardiac Intensive Care Unit at the hospital," I explained.

"Oh..." He leaned back against the pillow. After contemplating all this for a few seconds, he looked at me and asked in his secretive voice: "What happened?"

In as simple an explanation I could give, I said, "Your heart stopped beating. Paramedics got it going again and you've been here ever since." And to save him from having to ask the next obvious question I added: "You had 26 minutes of CPR."

His face showed surprise then disbelief as the news sunk in. He nodded thoughtfully as he digested this tidbit of news. "Wow!"

His eyebrows furrowed as he asked yet another question, trying to piece the information together.

"How long have I been here?"

"It's Monday morning. You've been here since Saturday," I answered.

"Oh." He closed his eyes, exhausted from his ordeal, and slept.

Chapter 28

Shortly thereafter, Dr. Hathaway walked briskly into Jeff's room. He was astounded by what he saw. He checked his chart, checked Jeff's vital signs, and then spoke. "Mr. Lyons, how are you feeling?"

Jeff answered, his voice raspy and deep, "Like I should be in the hospital."

I smiled, overjoyed at his sense of humor and quick wit showing the important signs of a full mental recovery. I said, "Dr. Hathaway, what do you think of this? God's done a miracle!"

The doctor was apparently surprised by the unexpected change of Jeff's situation. Was he also attributing it to a miracle of God? I couldn't be sure, but I knew he would be keeping a close watch on this particular patient.

After he left, Jeff gazed around his room then asked, "What happened?"

Once again, I answered, as if for the first time. And once again, with each of my answers he contemplated the information thoughtfully, as if he'd heard this story for the first time. He had an astounded look on his face when I told him once more that he'd survived 26 minutes of CPR.

An hour later, he asked the same questions once more. Patiently, I repeated what had happened. However, I became alarmed and wondered to myself, "Is this normal?"

When the nurse came to check Jeff's vital signs, I explained to her what was troubling me, then asked, "Is this normal?" I tried to not allow concern to enter into my question.

"Yes, this is very typical," she said, her words alleviating my dread. "The drugs that he's been on have a slight amnesia effect. He won't remember a lot of what happened. Be patient, he'll come around."

I was glad to answer his questions one hundred times over, but it was a relief to know his memory loss was temporary, a result of medications, and not due to damaged brain function.

Since it was Monday, I knew the number of visitors today would be diminished. The first to stop were Rick and Amy on their way to work. "It's good to see you, Jeff!" Rick heartily exclaimed.

"It's good to be seen," Jeff countered. His dry sense of humor certainly wasn't affected by his loss of memory.

Our friends who were keeping the boys took the day off and after breakfast, came to the hospital. The reunion of Jeff and his sons was heartwarming! Just 48 hours ago they had laid their eyes on Jeff lying in bed, in a coma, not knowing what the future held. Now it was joy, smiles, and relief.

Sam, Josh, and Micah were practically exploding with happiness. Never having dealt with a crisis of this magnitude, their deep cries to God the last two days were unparalleled. And God's answer had been resounding.

As they visited, I remembered something. Reaching into the bag holding my overnight items, I pulled out Jeff's reading glasses, those Josh had packed in faith on Saturday. I laid them on the table next to the three hand-drawn cards. The cards were a visible reminder of child-like faith, the glasses of unyielding faith.

These young men would be forever changed by this experience. We all would.

Chapter 29

Jeff was doing so well that he was soon upgraded to solid food. His first full meal in 2 ½ days was lasagna and a fruit salad. He was sitting up, enjoying his food and chatting with some visitors in his gravelly voice when Whitney, our EMT from Saturday morning, walked quietly into the room. She and her crew had just brought a patient to the ER, and before heading back to the station she had come up to check on Jeff and encourage me. I turned to greet her when I noticed her expression go from businesslike to astounded! She came fully expecting to find Jeff unresponsive.

A small gasp and high-pitched "Ahhhh!!" came from her mouth. "This is the best thing that's happened to me all year!" she exclaimed. "I can't believe it! I've got to tell the rest of the crew!" Whitney left as quickly as she had entered, and the energy in her step was unmistakable.

Later that afternoon, Whitney returned with Jamile, her EMS partner. Both walked into Jeff's room and introduced themselves as his paramedics. Jamile had not seen Jeff since Saturday morning at the Emergency Room. He gazed at him with a mixture of amazement and disbelief. I explained to Jeff that these two had been part of the large team that had continued CPR for 26 minutes. "They are part of the reason you are alive," I concluded.

Jeff regarded them both as I filled him in on these details. After hearing of their involvement he dryly stated, "Thank you for your perseverance!" We all laughed at his remark. Then the two shared from their perspective how God had been at work in the midst of our crisis.

"Believe it or not, you are an answer to *our* prayers," said Jamile. "When Whitney and I were first partnered, we realized we had a common faith. We recognized God as the ultimate healer, so before we even leave the station, it has become our habit to ask God to go before us into whatever situation we are heading. On our way we further request that he gives us understanding and wisdom to know just how to use the skills we have to take care of our patients.

"We were advised you were experiencing a possible heart attack, but were not expecting a full cardiac arrest. There were three teams working on you. We switched off after every minute. After the first few minutes, if a patient hasn't revived, the chances get pretty dismal."

Whitney chimed in, "We did all we could to resuscitate you, including five shocks to get your heart going again. We'd assumed we'd lost you, but when your heart started beating again after such a long time, we were all amazed."

"And," Jamile concluded, "not only did your heart start beating again, but your pulse and blood pressure were normal. That in itself is amazing. We knew it had to have been God answering our prayers. There's really no other explanation."

Looking into their faces, seeing their joy and amazement, I couldn't help but marvel that Jeff's recovery effected more than our family. God was inspiring people who were involved in different facets of his story. He had powerfully answered the request of Whitney and Jamile by giving them insight and faith to keep trying to revive Jeff. On future medical calls, these two would continue to pray, but now with greater expectation.

A profound truth was dawning on me. While I waited alone in my living room Saturday morning, almost paralyzed by shock and disbelief, God was responding to my desperate cries for help. He began orchestrating people and instilling in them faith that they didn't realize they had until thrust into those critical minutes.

How could I have known that a cadre of close friends, medical staff, and perfect strangers were involved in big and small ways to impact the outcome of Jeff's crisis? Yet God's firm and gentle hand was upon each and every one.

As a verse in the book of Habakkuk of the Old Testament recalls, *"Wonder and be astounded. For I am doing a work in your days that you would not believe if told."(ESV)*

Part 2

Now faith is the assurance of things hoped for, the conviction of things not seen.

Hebrews Chapter 11, verse 1 (ESV)

Chapter 30

I made one frantic phone call to my friend and pastor's wife, Amy. She assured me that she and Rick would be on their way quickly. When I spoke with her, I was afraid that Jeff had died, even as I hoped desperately for God's intervention. As the minutes ticked by, my frail optimism flagged. Despite the tender and insightful prayers of my neighbor, Phyllis, I began a heartbreaking mental transition, thinking of my future as a widow and mother to three fatherless teenaged boys. But God had other plans.

ക്ക്ക്ക്ക്ക്ക്ക്ക്ക്ക്ക്ക്ക്ക്ക്ക്

7:54 a.m.

Despite being stunned by the news I had just conveyed to her, Amy began making all-important phone calls to key members of Gateway Church. A dear and beloved member of the congregation had just died. His family would need support. Word needed to be spread. Three teenaged boys and a now single mother needed them.

"Oh, God.... NO!!!" Amy's mind screamed.

"Jay? This is Amy. Sue just called to pass on terrible news that Jeff's heart stopped beating. Paramedics are performing CPR but she thinks he has gone on to be with Jesus. Let your family know so they can pray for the Lyons family."

And so went the phone calls. Amy knew the message would be spread from home to home, person to person, the situation lifted up in prayer. In less than an hour, every family that attended Gateway regularly would know what had happened. Being a generous group, they would see to it that all of the Lyons' practical needs would be met, today and into the upcoming months.

After hanging up the phone, Amy was overcome with emotion. Then as she dressed in preparation for the trip to comfort me, her mind snapped to action. Welling up within her was a message that she voiced with conviction: "No! Satan, you cannot have him!! Jeff will live!"

Rick walked in the front door to the sound of Amy's loud and authoritative voice.

What is going on here?" he asked, watching his normally jovial wife stomping through the house and yelling.

As Amy shared the information she had heard from me, Rick also prepared to drive to our house. Together they stood in faith that Jeff had not died and summoned the power of God to respond and give him life.

❧❧❧❧❧❧❧❧❧❧❧❧❧❧❧❧

7:55 a.m.

On their way to a week of summer vacation at a lake house, Jay and his niece, Ivania, had just pulled into a truck stop

86

for a break. Other members of their large family would also be travelling to the lake today. Since all of them led busy lives, this time would be a great way to enjoy one another's company and reconnect. The early summer forecast for a sunny and warm week was an added bonus.

The cell phone rang.

"I wonder what Amy would want this morning?" Jay spoke with curiosity. His brow furrowed as he heard the news as I had spoken it to Amy minutes earlier.

Ending the call, Jay looked at Ivania, then shared with her the unexpected report.

He put forth this question: "What do you think God wants us to do with this?" Ivania wondered herself.

After a moment Jay spoke. "I have just finished studying the story of Lazarus being raised from the dead by Jesus. He called out Lazarus by name. If that model is good enough for Jesus, I think its good enough for us!"

In the middle of a truck stop in Georgia, two more of our faithful friends lifted their voices to Heaven: "Jeff, you will not die, but live! God, right at this moment, restore Jeff's spirit to his body."

❧❧❧❧❧❧❧❧❧❧❧❧❧❧❧❧❧

7:57 a.m.

The morning mist was rising from the surface of Lake Burton, Georgia, calm and quiet. Jay's twenty-six-year-old son, Stefan, was enjoying the peaceful morning when his cell phone rang and the heartbreaking message relayed. He fell to his knees, grieved to think one of his dearest spiritual mentors had died.

Stefan gathered his thoughts and prepared to intercede on our behalf, then abruptly stopped. Something deep in his soul resonated so strongly he couldn't ignore it. The Holy Spirit of God forbade him to pray for comfort in Jeff's death. Instead a fire burned within him to intercede for Jeff's life.

Stefan resolved to stay on his knees, praying for Jeff's life until he heard an update that would cause him to pray differently.

ۻۻۻۻۻۻۻۻۻۻۻۻۻۻۻۻ

8:00 a.m.

Tad received the news. As he conveyed the message to his wife, Laura, she doubled over, weeping with sorrow. Jeff was a close friend. Our families had camped, shared meals, and laughed together often. The men and boys practiced together on a firing range, knowing a Navy SEAL had honed his skills on that exact spot. Their family was dear to us and ours to them.

Tad's faith and convictions were ready to kick in powerfully.

With his eyes riveted on his wife, he spoke. "Laura. Jeff's not dead until God says he's dead. Until that time, we need to stand in faith for what God will do in Jeff's body."

In a living room, in the mountains, husband and wife agreed with conviction that Jeff's life would continue until God took it and not a moment earlier.

❧❧❧❧❧❧❧❧❧❧❧❧❧❧❧❧❧

8:05 a.m.

Then, Tad made a phone call. He told Laura, "I've got to call Rick Bussey. He'll pray for a person to be raised from the dead! I need to pray with someone with faith like that."

After hearing the news, Rick shared the information concerning Jeff with his family. Rick's son, Caleb, the young man who went to pick up our boys Saturday morning, responded immediately. Though not certain if it was an audible voice or not, Caleb was confident God was communicating with him.

You are not to pray for comfort for his family due to his death. Instead, pray for his life. Jeff is going to live and he will be like Lazarus." The message continued: "*This has happened so you may see God's glory.*"

As he shared this with his mom and dad, all three began praying with certainly. "Jeff! Come back to life!"

❧❧❧❧❧❧❧❧❧❧❧❧❧❧❧❧❧

In the meantime, three teams of paramedics were trying desperately to revive their patient. Switching off every minute due to the exhausting nature of CPR, the group toiled on. Every few minutes, a shock from a defibrillator was interspersed with chest compressions to try to get the heart beating. It was looking bleak. Normally, if the patient hasn't revived after 20 minutes, CPR is halted and a coroner sent to the scene of the death.

On this morning, however, the man's heart was doing something unusual. It was enough to give them incentive to continue trying.

One paramedic happened to be a neighbor. Allen had just arrived home after a 24-hour shift with the nearby Asheville Fire Department. He heard the sirens, then the radio message of a cardiac arrest a few houses away, so he hurried to the scene to help. This man had a personal stake in the survival of his own neighbor.

Later, Allen would share with fellow neighbors that he had witnessed a miracle when Jeff's heart did begin beating again, 26 minutes after CPR was begun.

Chapter 31

Tuesday:

Jeff was entertaining everyone who came to see him. His usual response to "Jeff, it's so good to see you," was "It's good to be seen!"

To "How are you feeling?" he'd say: "Oh, pretty good for being in the hospital."

Everyone seemed to be relieved Jeff was recovering, and there was a great sense of joy as a steady flow of friends came throughout the next two days.

But one person continued to be troubled.

Dr. Hathaway entered as Jeff was making a humorous statement with a visitor. He looked at Jeff, watching the good-natured verbal sparring. Then he looked at me, incredulous.

"Is this what your husband is typically like?" he asked.

I laughed! Yes, this was Jeff, but usually guarded and a deep thinker, his interactions with these friends was a change from normal. I knew what the doctor was getting at: had Jeff's personality changed?

"Well," I said, choosing my words carefully, "maybe it's more accurate to say it's *more* of him! He's usually not this outgoing, but it's definitely his sense of humor. And at this point his memory for details from the past are better than mine! He can't remember last week, but he can remember events and people from 20 years ago!"

The doctor shook his head, amazed. As he did some medical observations, our friends filed out.

Satisfied, he addressed both of us. "Since you are doing so well, Mr. Lyons, I would like to do a heart catheterization tomorrow morning. We'll sedate you and pass a tiny catheter through the arteries that surround your heart. When we find a blockage and if it is small enough, we can insert a stent that will help the blood flow. I'll send an intern to explain the entire process to you. If you have any questions after that, I'd be glad to answer them. It will be early in the morning, most likely around 8:00 a.m."

He looked at me. "Mrs. Lyons, may I have a word with you?"

After stepping out into the main Cardiac ICU corridor Dr. Hathaway continued, "There is the possibility that your husband has several blockages. There is no better explanation for why his heart stopped. Stents are practical if the blockages are small and if there aren't very many of them. If the blockages are too great we will have to halt the catheterization and schedule open-heart surgery. Time is of the essence. That's why I have him scheduled early. I want to reduce the chances of another cardiac arrest. He most likely wouldn't survive another one.

"I'd like to keep your husband as calm and stress-free as possible. That's why I didn't bring this item up in the room. But for now, we'll hope the catheterization is all he needs." And with a friendly smile added, "And, Mrs. Lyons, remember to take care of yourself."

After Dr. Hathaway left, I wondered to myself, "All right, God. What now?"

So I did what had become my habit for the prior few evenings: I prayed, and read the Bible... and listened.

Chapter 32

The morning dawned and I felt a strong urge to ask my friends from Gateway and elsewhere to pray on Jeff's behalf. But he was scheduled for one of the earliest operating room times. The orderlies were on their way to take him to surgery. How was I to get the word out to more than just a handful of people? I wasn't even certain what to ask for. As the saying goes, *"God works in mysterious ways..."*

Just as they were preparing to roll him to surgery, one of the nurses looked at his medical chart and noticed that a crucial procedure had not been performed during the night. In the event a stent is inserted, a daily aspirin to reduce blood clots is required for the rest of that person's life. Jeff has an aspirin allergy, so an aspirin desensitization process should have been completed prior to the catheterization.

The doctor was informed and walked into Jeff's room obviously frustrated. The catheterization was postponed until 4:30 p.m. and the aspirin regimen begun, which would require most of the day to complete.

Dr. Hathaway may have been upset, but I recognized the delay as an opportunity to rally my friends to pray for a specific outcome. "OK, God. You've given us a window of opportunity. What do you want us to ask for?" His answer came to my mind in such a precise way that I knew it had to have been from the Lord. This is the petition I asked people to pray:

"Let the doctors see exactly what they need to. But if there are no blockages in Jeff's arteries, that they would give God the credit." In other words, I didn't want to be foolish; if there were blocked arteries, by all means, I wanted the doctors to see them. But since the best cardiologist in the area was convinced of at least one obstruction, if there were none, wouldn't that mean God had again stepped in and performed yet another miracle in response to his believing people?

Once again, word spread. Texts, emails, and phone calls were made. People assured us that they would pray according to my request. As the afternoon wore on, I felt a strong sense of God's favor resting on our pleas.

Precisely at 4:30 p.m., the orderly came for Jeff. This time, however, I had a deep sense of expectation that God would receive praise. This afternoon just a small handful of friends sat with me in the waiting room. After all, it was the middle of the week and most of my friends held full-time jobs.

While waiting, we prayed. Our greatest desire, other than for Jeff to be safe, was for people to understand the power and goodness of God. Shortly, four different neighbors happened to stop in. They had not been to the hospital since Jeff had been admitted. They had just heard the news and were stopping in to visit and hear the story of Jeff's amazing recovery. Having had no idea that he was in the midst of a heart catheterization, they too waited with us.

As I told the story and relived the remarkable move of God's power I was suddenly filled with abundant joy, energy, and faith. I stated that when the doctor came to say that he couldn't find anything, that I would have a hard time containing my exuberance! Everyone in that waiting room was filled with expectation. How would our prayers be realized?

We didn't have long to wait. "Family with Jeffrey Lyons?" the cardiologist called. I jumped up, strode to him with a smile on my face. "I'm Mrs. Lyons."

The doctor seemed perplexed. "I don't understand it. We couldn't find a thing wrong with your husband's arteries. His heart is in great shape. If I didn't know any better, I would have never expected that he'd had any heart problems. His cholesterol and all of his bloodwork is good. And, the paramedics that did CPR on your husband did the best that I think I've ever seen. They deserve a lot of credit for the fact your husband is still with us."

"Thank you, God!" I exclaimed. Then I looked at the doctor and surmised, "You know, a lot of people have been praying that God would remove the blockages from Jeff's heart. Could it be you have witnessed a miracle? God seems to be doing that a lot with Jeff lately."

The doctor smiled and said non–committedly, "It could be." He wheeled Jeff to his room to recover and left the rest of us to rejoice.

Chapter 33

In the midst of our celebration, I saw a familiar form striding toward us. "Dr. Hathaway!" I said with exuberance. "Have you heard the good news?!"

Of course he had. Appearing to be a bit distracted, he shared from his point of view: "Yes, I've heard. It may be good news to you, but not to me…." then checked his words. "Let me rephrase that. It *is* good news, but it leaves me with a dilemma; it still doesn't help me explain why your husband's heart stopped beating."

"I can tell you what happened!" I said enthusiastically.

The doctor regarded me brimming with joy, a wife hardly able to contain her excitement. With a good-natured grin on his face he prompted: "Ok, Mrs. Lyons… why don't you fill me in."

Not wanting to appear disrespectful of this man's great ability and expertise, yet also desiring to credit a supernatural move of God, I shared simply, "You've done everything perfectly. I just happen to believe that God went before you and supernaturally healed Jeff's heart."

Listening to my explanation didn't remove his dilemma. He gave a quick, laughing exhale. "Even if what you say is true, my CEO wouldn't accept that in my report!" More seriously he continued, "There is something in your husband's heart that caused it to stop. It's only a matter of finding it. My job is to unearth the cause."

Looking at his watch Dr. Hathaway said, "It's already too late for today, but I will order an MRI for tomorrow morning. That will show us if there is a part of the heart not moving properly or getting a poor blood supply. There is a chance there is scar tissue affecting the rhythm. The MRI will certainly show us what the problem is." With that, he excused himself and continued his rounds.

Returning to Jeff's bedside, waiting for him to revive from his surgery, I related my conversation with Dr. Hathaway to Kendall. She laughed and quipped, "And I don't think any respectable insurance agency would accept 'miraculous healing' as a cure, either!"

Dr. Hathaway was prudent to weed out every possible cause of Jeff's cardiac arrest, but in my heart I knew God would get all of the glory when he failed to find anything.

Chapter 34

Wednesday:

Jeff continued to get better. In the morning he was assisted to a reclining chair in the room. It was his first time out of bed. He handled it well, another step in his recovery. Still quite weak, he was returned to his bed after an hour.

Then a wiry man with a graying and receding hairline, button-down shirt, blue jeans, and tears in his eyes entered the room hesitantly. The first words I heard him utter were: "This is Jeff. My, oh, my, it's good to see you!"

After gazing at Jeff, the gentleman turned his attention to me. "You don't recognize me, do you?" he asked with a shy smile.

To be truthful, he looked vaguely familiar, but I could not recall where I'd see him.

"I'm the chaplain from the fire department, Wilson Bishop." He leaned toward me and engulfed my hand in both of his with a warm handshake.

Then I remembered. Saturday morning he'd worn a ball cap with the words "Fire Department Chaplain" emblazoned on the front.

With an easy drawl, typical of the people who grew up in the southern Appalachian Mountains, he said, "Monday afternoon, Whitney came back to the department and practically exploded into the station with the news that you were sitting up, eating lasagna, and talking! All of us were overwhelmed. Before you knew it, we were all praising the Lord! Most of us who work at that station are believers, you know. But we've never experienced anything like this," the chaplain marveled.

Mr. Bishop gazed at Jeff. "Mr. Lyons, I just had to come see you. I hope you don't mind."

Jeff assured him that we didn't mind. We were grateful for his prayers and concern on that morning.

He looked at me again. "Do you remember what I told you when Jeff was being taken out of your house? I said we'd hear a good report." At that memory his eyes glistened with moisture. He was struggling to maintain his composure.

"Mrs. Lyons, you have to understand that I never make promises like that. Everything about Saturday morning was completely untypical of me," he emphasized.

Chaplain Bishop launched into a narrative that shared a part of the story that we couldn't have known while we were in the midst of Jeff's crisis. It was another instance of overwhelming faith making a difference.

"I usually keep my radio off Saturday mornings," he began. "If the Chief needs me, he'll call the house. But this last Saturday, for some reason, I switched it on. Almost right away I heard the call of a possible heart attack in the Bent Creek neighborhood. I can't explain it, Mrs. Lyons, but I told my wife,

'Neesy, I have *got* to go on that call.' And she'll tell you that I never do that, either.

"I grabbed my radio, got in my truck, and headed your way. Now, we only live a few minutes from your neighborhood, so I got there fast, but then didn't know what house to go to! I got the address and pulled up onto your street not long after the rest of the crew got there."

The chaplain looked at me once more. "When I walked into your house, you may remember I said 'I'd like to pray for your husband in Jesus' name, because his is the only one I know that is powerful enough to heal your husband.' You've got to know that I am never that bold. I'm shy and quiet. I don't even pray with a family until I'm invited to first. I need to respect people's privacy and their faith, which may be different than mine. But I sensed a similar faith in your home before I even spoke with you."

Amazement on his face as he relived his story, Mr. Bishop went on: "But as I said already, everything about Saturday was different. I had a boldness in my prayer for Jeff that I have never experienced before. Then after I told you 'we *will* hear a good report on your husband', I thought: 'What have I done? I just made a promise to that poor wife that's out of my control! I can't give someone false hope.'

"So I drove home and told my wife, 'Neesy, I need to call the boys at the church and get together for a special meeting.

We've got to ask God to do what I promised he would do for that poor wife!'

"And that's what I did. My brother's the pastor there. We all got together and had a prayer meeting right then on Saturday afternoon. Then on Sunday, the whole church stopped what we were doing and had a prayer service for you. People were weeping and praying in agreement for God to heal you, Jeff.

"The Bible verse we prayed was Jeremiah 17:14. *'Heal me, oh Lord and I shall be healed; save me, and I shall be saved, for you are my praise.'* That's a powerful verse and we believed it with our whole hearts.

"At that time I didn't even know what your name was. When Whitney came into the station with the news, I burst out in tears. God is so good! I can't hardly keep a dry eye when I think of how good he is." Mr. Bishop removed a small white handkerchief from his back pocket and dabbed his eyes.

"You are a miracle, Jeff. I will never forget what God did for you." He finished with, "I just had to see you for myself and let you know my story." With that, he grasped my hand again. But a handshake wasn't enough to express my gratitude, so I hugged this dear man and asked him to thank his wife and church for standing with us.

After he left, I recalled my initial response to the chaplain. I had felt he was an intruder on my personal grief. Little did I know that he was a vital piece of God's tapestry, woven together with a multitude of other believers that God put in place on Jeff's behalf. The members of Mr. Bishop's church congregation, Words of Life Tabernacle, were praying for Jeff at the same time as the members of our church, adding prayers upon prayers.

God had set in motion a set of circumstances before I had any strength or understanding to ask. Another Bible verse came to my mind: *"God knows your needs before you even ask...."*

And with that realization, I sobbed with gratefulness.

Chapter 35

How else had God intervened in our crisis? I thought back to Josh's recollection of his initial trip to the hospital and noticing the words "I AM" on the reusable shopping bag. Was it a supernatural event or just a coincidence? By itself, this occurrence wasn't very convincing. Combined with all the other instances, however, a pattern was emerging that deepened my assurance of God's involvement and answers to multitudes of prayers.

After Chaplain Bishop's visit and while Jeff was napping, I made a trip to the parking garage where our van had been left for my use in the event I needed it. Unlocking the doors and sliding the side door open, I located the bag, still in its original location, in a gap between the middle seats. I looked more closely at the iPlay bag, expecting the words "I AM" to be absolutely unmistakable. Moving to the back seat and positioning myself where Josh would have been sitting, I was astounded to find there was only one way the bag could be situated in order for him to see those two words. Even a variation of a few inches would make it virtually unnoticeable. After all, this phrase was just one of twenty.

Recalling my time in the Emergency Room waiting room, hadn't I asked the Lord to give my sons faith, not fear, when picked up by our friends Saturday morning? Why should I be surprised when he answered?

Then I remembered my inability to contact certain friends on Saturday morning. I was jolted when I recognized that perhaps I *had* to contact Amy. How could the end result have differed if Jay and Ivania, Tad and Laura, or Caleb's family hadn't interceded for Jeff? Again I asked myself: was this just another coincidence, or had God himself put in motion this sequence of events?

Certainly, as I had read hundreds of times, *"Nothing is impossible with God."*

Phone calls, Chaplain Bishop's actions, a shopping bag, and who knows how many other details had been attended to by our loving God. I closed my eyes and thanked him for being involved.

"God, you are so kind. And big. And powerful. Thank you for instilling faith in Josh and reassuring him during a stressful and uncertain time. Thank you for causing me to call Amy Saturday morning. Give Wilson Bishop more opportunities to use his gift of faith to encourage hurting and distressed families.

"And God? Let this whole situation be for your glory."

Chapter 36

Wednesday afternoon:

Jeff was dealing with a consistent cough, common after the removal of a breathing tube. It's the body's response and healing from the intrusion of forced oxygen. To someone whose sternum and ribs were broken as the result of CPR, a nagging cough can be excruciating. Every small cough caused him pain, and though holding a pillow to his chest helped, it was still agonizing.

Not only that, but the MRI Dr. Hathaway ordered was ready to be administered. An MRI takes almost a half-hour to complete and requires the patient's complete stillness for the image to be clear. Jeff couldn't cough for the entire time of the procedure or they would have to do it again.

Reminded that nothing is too big or small for God, my prayer was for Jeff to be comfortable and able to suppress his coughing for the duration of the imaging. When Jeff returned to his bed an hour later, I found that once again God had responded. He didn't cough once during the procedure.

The result from the MRI? The technician reading the results could not find anything wrong with Jeff's heart. Once again, Dr. Hathaway came to inform me of this result. This time I didn't even say a word. I didn't have to. I just smiled.

"I know exactly what you're thinking," he said with some frustration in his voice. "After my shift is complete, I am going to personally go over that MRI millimeter by millimeter! There is something in Jeff's heart that caused it to stop and I am determined to find it." With that promise, he left.

I found myself honored by the effort our cardiologist was willing to invest in our case. He had taken an interest in Jeff as his patient, devoting great energy and attention to detail. His tenacity and desire to unearth every possibility, combined with years of expertise, most likely earned him the coveted position of Chief Medical Officer of Mission Memorial Hospital. Personally, I was grateful God had seen fit to place Dr. William Hathaway in the Cardiac ICU last Sunday morning. I felt confident God would help him see exactly what he needed to.

Chapter 37

Sunday morning, four days later and eight days after Jeff's cardiac arrest: 11:00 a.m.

The sanctuary was full. People were gathered with a great expectation. God had answered their prayers in a spectacular and miraculous way on behalf of a friend and fellow church member on the verge of death. Some would agree that he had been resurrected from death by the powerful intervention of God. Hearts were full of joy and everyone was looking forward to releasing that exuberance to heaven in song and praise.

The rear door squeaked open and made a dull thud as it closed. A gasp of joy escaped from the mouth of one church member. Then a burst of clapping. All heads turned, and with one accord the congregation stood to its feet. Spontaneous applause, cheering, and shouts of praise erupted. Joy and wonder were unmistakable on every face as Jeff walked slowly, weakly, but deliberately toward some seats near the front.

Pastor Will, with a huge smile on his face, asked all to join in worship. Everyone turned their attention to the one worthy of praise, the source of Jeff's life and amazing recovery. Joyful music filled the building as Alex, Patrick, and the worship team led us all in a magnificent time of adoration and devotion.

As the sanctuary resounded with joyful music, I quickly stepped out into the hall and made a phone call. Words of Life Tabernacle, the church home of Chaplain Wilson Bishop, would also be in the midst of their Sunday morning service. As the call connected, I spoke with happiness and gratefulness for this church body that also stood in faith: "This is Sue Lyons. You all prayed for my husband's life last Sunday. Please let Mr. Bishop and your members know that at this moment, Jeff is standing in church and praising the Lord! Thank you, all!"

Barely able to contain my excitement, I returned to the sanctuary and raised my own hands toward heaven as we sang our praises to God.

Timeline:

Saturday morning:

- At approximately 7:35 I found Jeff unresponsive in our den and called 9-1-1.
- 7:36: Whitney and Jamile prayed for the man they were going to care for.
- 7:46: EMS arrived at our house.
- 7:48: Whitney and Jamile began CPR.
- 7:50: More EMS teams arrived at our home.
- 7: 52: I called Rick and Amy.
- 7:54- 8:10: Phone calls were made to church members.
- 7:54: My neighbor Phyllis came.
- 8:00: The Fire Department Chaplain arrived.
- 8:14: Jeff's heart began beating on its own.

Sunday:

- 7:15 p.m.: The coma-inducing drugs were stopped and Jeff woke up twenty minutes later with no apparent brain damage.

Monday:

- Convinced of blocked arteries and concerned about another heart attack, Dr. Hathaway scheduled a heart catheterization for early Tuesday morning.

Tuesday:

- 8:00 a.m. An intern came to take Jeff for his heart catheterization. His nurses realized he needed an aspirin desensitization regimen. The catheterization was rescheduled to 4:30 p.m.
- 5:00 p.m.: The heart catheterization showed clear arteries.

Wednesday:

- Noon: The technician interpreting the MRI found no heart damage.
- Late Wednesday night: The MRI results were confirmed by Dr. Hathaway. He did find minimal damage in an area of the heart that would not affect function.

Saturday evening:

- Jeff was released from the hospital.

Postscript:

Naturally, we want to know the steps necessary to achieve favor with God, especially in the realm of prayer. I, too, have wondered many times over the years why God has not answered certain pleas. They were unselfish and offered on behalf of dear people in the midst of deep struggle, pain, or hardship. Yet they seemed to go unanswered. Did I need to pray more? Fast more? Have more faith? Was I doing something wrong that put a wedge between myself and God? Heartbreaking questions. Deep and honest questions. Faith-testing questions.

Why does God seem to answer some prayers and not others? Is there a formula? We all wish there was, but I haven't found one. And I'm glad because that would lift the burden from God and put it on me, a heavy load to bear. Without doubt, I do trust that our prayers are not in vain and that God has purpose in all we go through no matter the outcome here on this earth.

The Bible explains that as we draw near to God, he will draw near to us. As Whitney and Jamile, Rick and Amy, Tad and Laura, Jay and Ivania, Caleb, Chaplain Bishop, my sons, and others listened to and responded to the whisper and clear direction of God's spirit, a cascade of events followed. Draw near to God and respond to his promptings without fear or hesitancy. Trust that his ways are good, confident that he hears our cries and cares about us in our pain as well as in our joy.

"This is not your own doing, it is the gift of God... that no one may boast." And, *"Though many, (we) are one body in Christ, and individually members of one another." Ephesians 2:8 and Romans 12:5 (ESV)*

This is not my story or Jeff's story but God's. God, in his mercy, wisdom, and deep love, gave us one another to be a body, not made out of flesh and bone, but out of a common love and commitment to serve him and one another.

Two members of this body prayed and asked God to go before them as the healer. Several responded to God's promptings and prayed, not for comfort to a widow, but life for their friend. Compelled by a power that was irresistible, one member of this same body of Christ drove to the scene of an imminent death only to promise the impractical and walk in a faith he never knew he had. In Florida, another part of the body led a worship service asking for healing on behalf of her blood brother.

How many prayed? How many fasted? How many worshipped at home, on their knees begging God for his mercy and healing? We will certainly never know in this lifetime.

But we do know that God, in his great mercy, responded. Jeff's heart started beating after 26 minutes of CPR. Father's Day evening was the greatest breakthrough for three teenage boys and a wife, as Jeff arose out of a coma with no adverse side-effects. The mystery of no heart or brain damage, clear arteries, and a full recovery after the matter of a few days may cause the medical world to scratch their heads. The release date of "30 days" was erased from the whiteboard, and Jeff walked out of the hospital one week after he entered.

Tad's admonition from the beginning will always be with me as a reminder and an encouragement: "The doctors may have a diagnosis, but God always has the final say."

And I say… To God be the Glory! Amen

In case you were wondering…..

Since Jeff's brush with death and miraculous recovery, we have had many occasions to share his story with friends and acquaintances. Similar questions arise concerning his cardiac arrest, resulting time in the hospital, and since. You may be wondering the same things yourself. Here are our answers to the most commonly asked questions:

Does Jeff remember anything that happened to him the day of his cardiac arrest?

Jeff doesn't remember anything of that morning. That is probably a good thing, since it was traumatic and painful. He has snippets of memories of the days leading up to his episode. In a humorous vein, he remembers everything about our vacation the week before! Wouldn't it be great if all of us had that kind of selective memory? Another interesting point is he doesn't recall any of his time in the hospital, despite the fact he was mentally sharp and witty. Our friends in the medical field attribute this to the powerful medications administered; some have amnesia inducing side-effects.

Did he have an out-of-body experience?

Most people are surprised and disappointed that Jeff doesn't have a recollection of any kind of supernatural experience.

Have the doctors ever found anything wrong with his heart?

The cardiologists have yet to find any problems with Jeff's heart. In the intervening months, he has had several check-ups with no sign of disease or heart-related issues.

How has this event changed you?

As you might imagine, Jeff has a new perspective on life and death! One of his favorite stories is about a man at the ocean walking on the beach with God. The Lord points out that each grain of sand on this beach represents a year of eternity. And not just this beach, but all of the beaches in the world combined. Then God stoops down and picks up a tiny pinch of sand between his fingers and comments, "This little bit of sand represents the years of your life. Will you entrust me with these few years?"

The man's eyes take in the scope of the size of the beach, then rest on the tiny amount of sand in God's hand. "Of course," the man answers. "How could I deny you such a small time?"

God further inquired, "What if these years are hard? What if they are painful? May I still have your permission to work in your life according to what I see is best?"

Jeff points out that when we are in the midst of difficult circumstances those grains of sand appear to us as boulders. But in the hands of a loving God, there is a completely new perspective.

We trust God in spite of circumstances and do our best to encourage those who are themselves in the midst of crisis.

Why do you think this happened to you?

God likes to use everyday people to declare his might. We hope that as others hear our story, they recognize God is at work in every situation, even the difficult ones. He does hear our cries to him; he cares about us.

Our deepest desire is that people of faith will learn to call upon God, asking him to reveal to them how to respond when they or others are in the midst of tragedy. *"God, how do you want me to respond to this?"* is one of our first prayers now. And in the event he asks us to pray in faith for a miracle, we do. Be prepared, since he may ask the same of you! Although, sometimes God only wants us to sit quietly in the waiting room with a friend, hold a baby, or provide a meal.

Our church, Gateway, has changed, too. People who were a part of this event have greater boldness to believe God for a miracle. They share Jeff's story with enthusiasm. And no one goes through a crisis alone.

Our question to you:

Has this story challenged you? How are you to respond?

May our God, the mighty Savior, bless you, guide you, and change you forever!

Jeff and Sue Lyons

117

Acknowledgements:

Now that you have read the story, I would like to recognize some groups of people because they deserve to be applauded:

First, to paramedics, Emergency Room, and Intensive Care medical staff everywhere who work day in and day out to save lives. I hope more people value your perseverance, expertise, and kindness.

Next, to fire and police department chaplains. You have the excruciatingly difficult task of comforting family members and close friends in the face of deep emotional pain and loss. Your presence and care does make a difference, even if you don't recognize it at the time.

And to those who prayed, believed for a miracle, loved, and supported us. Your sacrifices literally changed our lives and the ultimate outcome.

From start to finish I had a team of supporters. Thank you, Julie McConnell, for being my biggest cheerleader and for inspiring me to write this story. Without you I may never have gotten beyond page 1. Jon Brooks, in my mind's eye I can imagine you at your sink with tears in your eyes after reading the first few pages. Your message of "This story has got to be told," gave me the encouragement I needed; shortly thereafter the words just seemed to fall into place. Thanks to Adair Brooks, Rick Brunson, and John Parrish, for your editing expertise.

Sam, Josh, and Micah: I am proud to call you my sons! Thank you for giving me the time I needed to work on this book.

And Jeff, I look forward to sharing the rest of the story with you!

Has this story touched you in any way? We would love to hear about it! Please visit our website: www.26theBook.com

www.ingramcontent.com/pod-product-compliance
Lightning Source LLC
Chambersburg PA
CBHW061740020426
42331CB00006B/1306